ELECTIONS and the MASS MEDIA

Developed by
DAVID BLOMQUIST
Harvard University

Data in this unit were made available from the 1980 National Election Study by the Center for Political Studies of the University of Michigan. The Inter-University Consortium for Political and Social Research provides access to these data.

The American Political Science Association
1527 New Hampshire Avenue, N.W.
Washington, D.C. 20036
1981

Poynter Institute for Media Studies
Library

AUG 1 7 '87

This SETUPS has been reviewed by political scientists with expertise in the field of election studies. The reviews have been used by the author in revising the manuscript.

Elections and the Mass Media is published under the auspices of the APSA's Office of Educational Affairs. The views expressed are those of the author, and not of the American Political Science Association.

Copyright © 1982 by the American Political Science Association, 1527 New Hampshire Avenue, N.W., Washington, D.C., 20036, under International and Pan-American Copyright Conventions. All rights reserved. No part of this book may be reproduced in any form or by any means without permission in writing from the publisher.

Set in Optima Medium by the Harvard University Printing Office, Boston, Massachusetts. Printed in the United States of America.

ISBN 0-915654-51-2

Foreword

The SETUPS have proven to be an enormously useful and popular tool for introducing social science students to data analysis, recent research studies, and using computers. Approximately 50,000 copies have been ordered for classes by faculty in more than 250 colleges and universities in the United States, Canada, Australia, and Europe.

The SETUPS were initiated with the support of grants from the National Science Foundation. The SETUPS format was established originally by faculty working together in "college faculty workshops." Once their utility was established, the Steering Committee for the political science undergraduate education project invited faculty working at their own institutions to develop other SETUPS units. At the close of the grant period, the American Political Science Association and the Inter-University Consortium for Political and Social Research agreed to a procedure to provide faculty with assistance and incentives to prepare new SETUPS.

With the publication of *Elections and the Mass Media*, faculty and students engaged in research on American electoral behavior will have a dataset and resource on the most recent national election.

SETUPS: American Politics

The SETUPS in this series were designed for use in courses on American government and public policy analysis. During a testing period they were widely used in these courses, and found to be helpful in advanced courses as well. Data in the form of OSIRIS, SPSS or card image for all SETUPS is provided by the Inter-University Consortium for Political and Social Research, University of Michigan, without charge through an agreement with the American Political Science Association, for each order of 25 or more SETUPS.

Other SETUPS in the American Politics series currently available are:

Voting Behavior: The 1980 Election, By Bruce D. Bowen, C. Anthony Broh and Charles L. Prysby.
Political Socialization Across the Generations, by Paul Allen Beck, Jere W. Bruner and L. Douglas Dobson.
Political Participation, by F. Christopher Arterton and Harlan Hahn.
The Supreme Court in American Politics: Policy Through Law, 2nd edition, by John Paul Ryan and C. Neal Tate.
U.S. Energy, Environment and Economic Problems: A Public Policy Simulation, by Barry Hughes.
The Dynamics of Political Budgeting: A Public Policy Simulation, by Marvin K. Hoffman.
The Fear of Crime, by Wesley G. Skogan and William R. Klecka.

Acknowledgements

Even if only one name appears on the title page, every book is a group effort to some extent. This one is no exception.

Funding for the SETUPS program is provided by the American Political Science Association and the Inter-University Consortium for Political and Social Research. The Faculty of Arts and Sciences, Harvard University, also supported development of this manuscript. Sheilah Mann, the Association's educational affairs director, edited the text cheerfully and efficiently. Jerome Clubb, Carolyn Geda, and Pat Green were gracious hosts and helpful colleagues during my visit to the Consortium.

I am grateful for the comments and support of several reviewers: Doris Graber, at the University of Illinois-Chicago Circle; Jerome Katz, at the University of Pennsylvania; Michael J. Robinson, at Georgetown University; Mary Thornberry, at Davidson College; and at Harvard, Stephen J. Agostini, Leo D'Acierno, Christopher Damm, and Jonathan W. Kenton. In addition, Kenton assisted in preparation of the dataset and was responsible for the content analysis introduced in Chapter 3; Agostini executed the graph which accompanies Chapter 4.

Finally, this manuscript reflects the enthusiasm for empirical research imparted to me by Harvard's James A. Davis. I am especially thankful for his encouragement.

All of these individuals and organizations share in what is successful about this SETUPS. The blame for what is not rests solely with the single name on the title page.

Cambridge, Massachusetts
December, 1981

Contents

I. The potential and the reality   1
   1. Introduction   1
   2. From myth to Milquetoast   2
   3. From Milquetoast to. . .?   6

II. An introduction to empirical research   12
   1. What is empirical research?   12
   2. Contingency table analysis — two variables   16
   3. Contingency table analysis — many variables   19
   4. Writing the research report   22

III. Exercises   24
   1. Who uses the media?   24
   2. Concern for issues   25
   3. Agenda-setting   26
   4. Campaign participation   27
   5. Explaining the vote   28

IV. Toward a research agenda   29
   1. The press and voting behavior   29
   2. The press in the electoral process   32
   3. A conclusion — at a beginning   38

   Codebook   41

   References   6

I. The potential and the reality

Just after 8:15, the decision reached the anchor desk in the middle of NBC's Studio 8H in New York. With obvious pride in his organization's nimbleness, John Chancellor looked out at the cameras before him. Though Americans were still voting somewhere in nearly every state in the union, the NBC pundits had reached a verdict: Ronald Reagan, Chancellor declared, would be the next president of the United States.

Within 90 minutes, similar scorekeepers at ABC and CBS concurred, and an expressionless Jimmy Carter appeared before other cameras in a Washington hotel to acknowledge the end of his political career. An hour after Carter's concession, Reagan, spirited and confident, strolled before still other cameras in Los Angeles to savor victory. It was all over before most Americans retired to bed.

Yet at that point, the Reagan victory did not actually exist. Not a single vote had been certified by the state canvassing agencies. The Electoral College, in which the constitutitonal authority for selecting the president rested, would not convene in the various state capitals for three weeks, and the results of its balloting wouldn't be announced until the new Congress came to Washington in January. But the nation's broadcast networks, newspapers, and wire services had concluded that Reagan was the winner, and it is a measure of the power and faith entrusted to these organizations of mass communication that virtually everyone believed them.

Just a few months earlier, however, many people had gone to bed believing something else the mass media had told them about politics, only to receive a jolting surprise the next morning. "Gerald Ford will be (Reagan's) selection as his vice-presidential running mate," Walter Cronkite told the nation on the third night of the Republican National Convention. "They are going to come to this convention hall tonight to appear together on this platform...to announce that Ford will run with him" (quoted in Smith and Rudulph, 1980: 54). The next day's breakfast news told a different story: when Reagan finally came to the convention hall early that morning, it was to announce that George Bush would be his vice-presidential nominee.

Such periodic gaffes lead many Americans to express dissatisfaction with the institutions which tell them about the comings and goings of their world.

Perhaps as many as two-thirds of them agreed with former vice-president Spiro Agnew's assertion in 1969 that the news media had "grown fat and irresponsible" (Agnew, 1970: 80; Harris poll cited in Erikson and Luttbeg, 1973: 148). In 1980, according to one national survey, only 23 percent of Americans had substantial confidence in the news media (National Opinion Research Center, 1980: 107). Yet more of them were watching and reading than ever: in 1980, television news viewership stood at a record 52 million, and a near-record 62 million newspapers were being sold daily (personal communication, A.C. Nielsen Co., 1981; *Editor and Publisher*, 1980). No other nation consumes so much mass communication; in no other place is mass communication so inextricably linked to the electoral process.

This SETUPS examines the relationships between the press* and the voting public. We will consider how much influence news organizations have on the nation's political attitudes and on its choice of political leaders — or, rather, *you* will consider that influence, for in this unit, it will be up to *you* to ask the questions and find the answers.

This chapter will get you started by introducing briefly some of the most important research by social scientists working in this field. Succeeding chapters will show you how to conduct your own research — using the 1980 National Election Study, an extensive survey of the American electorate — to determine for yourself how influential the media are in politics, and to assess what difference such influence makes for the course of public policy.

2. From myth to Milquetoast

The media's influence on political behavior has been a most elusive research subject. It remains so, even after a half-century of intense investigation. There are few absolutes in mass communication research; the history of the field is a sequence of one generation's work being reversed by the next.

For centuries, kings, philosophers, and politicians all merely *assumed* that the press was a powerful force in shaping public opinion. Soon after William Caxton brought the printing press to England in 1476, government moved to contain it. In 1534, Henry VIII decreed that print shops could be established only with prior royal approval. Printers who produced material unfavorable to the Crown lost their licenses and were put out of business or imprisoned.

Two hundred years later, the press was widely reputed to be a critical element in provoking revolutionary fervor in America. The infamous Stamp Act of 1765 imposed a huge excise on colonial newspapers, which responded with pithy sarcasm and some of the first calls for public resistance. Much of the intellectual fuel for the fire came from the essays of Thomas Paine, carried as

---

*Some authors use "the press" to signify just the written mass media — that is, newspapers and magazines. Here and throughout, however, I use "the press" and "the mass media" interchangeably to refer to all the principal means of mass communication — newspapers, magazines, television, and radio. Two less-important modes of communication, motion pictures and books, are omitted from this discussion, though many of the observations made here apply to these other media as well.

editorials by newspapers throughout the colonies. Indeed, George Washington considered the press one of the revolution's most important allies; when the supply of linen used for manufacturing paper grew short during the war, Washington pleaded with patriot women to save any rags that might be shredded to make printing stock (Emery, 1972: 94).

If anything, the press's reputation as a leader of public opinion intensified as the republic matured. The Federalist papers of Hamilton, Madison, and Jay originally appeared as "op-ed" columns in a New York newspaper. William Lloyd Garrison's fiery *Liberator* and Horace Greeley's *Tribune* gave the abolitionist movement loud, impassioned, prominent voices; doubtless Abraham Lincoln was only half joking when he introduced Harriet Beecher Stowe, author of *Uncle Tom's Cabin*, as "the little woman who wrote the book that made this great war." And as the nation prepared to go to war with Spain in 1898, many believed it was the jingoistic bombast of William Randolph Hearst's *New York Journal* that goaded Congress and President McKinley into battle. Few would have disputed Walter Lippmann's assertion in 1919 that "the newspaper is...the book out of which a people determines its conduct" (1920: 47).

No wonder, then, that when departments of political science and sociology began to be established in American universities around the turn of the century, the press was one of the first subjects of inquiry. The very earliest works, such as the sociologist Robert Park's book on the immigrant press (1929), were largely descriptive. Perhaps the first systematic attempt to ascertain the political impact of the press appeared in Harold Gosnell's 1937 study of machine politics in Chicago. Gosnell undertook a statistical analysis — remarkably sophisticated for those pre-computer days — in which he attempted to relate social and economic characteristics and newspaper reading habits to election returns. Working only with census totals and precinct voting figures, Gosnell isolated several Chicago neighborhoods where the circulation and attitude of a newspaper were closely associated with the success of certain candidates. He identified three "typical situations' in which the newspapers' endorsements seemed to have the greatest impact:

> If (the newspapers) have followed a vigorous policy with reference to factional leaders in primary elections, they may be able to determine the fate of the candidates associated with these leaders. In general elections, if the papers have followed a consistent policy regarding a given party faction, they may be able to influence their readers to split their tickets in favor of, or in opposition to, that faction. Finally, if the press follows a tenacious policy during an economic crisis, it may be able to retard or prevent shifts from one major party to another. (Gosnell, 1937: 181)

Gosnell's findings provided social scientists with concrete evidence that the press was an important political actor. Further evidence seemed to be contained in the news from Europe, where the propaganda machine of Adolf Hitler appeared to have captured the minds of the German people. Many a social scientist winced at the brilliant yet frightening films of the Nazis' mass rallies.

For one social scientist, those films had special meaning. Paul Lazarsfeld, an associate professor of sociology at Columbia and director of that university's Office of Radio Research, was a refugee from German-dominated Vienna. His academic interest in the political power of mass communication was partly attributable, no doubt, to what he saw Hitler's newspapers, radio, and movies accomplishing in his homeland.

In 1940, Lazarsfeld and two of his associates, Bernard Berelson and Hazel Gaudet, set out to measure the repercussions of campaign press coverage on voting in an American presidential election. Unlike Gosnell, they decided not to rely on election and census records, but to employ the then-new techniques of opinion polling and ascertain voters' attitudes directly.

For convenience, Lazarsfeld, Berelson, and Gaudet decided to concentrate their study on a confined geographic space: Erie County, Ohio, a section of northern Ohio about equally divided between city (Sandusky) and farmland. From May to November, one of the Lazarsfeld team's interviewers visited someone once each month in every 20th house or apartment in Erie County — 600 people in all. They talked about political parties, candidates, issues, and the news.

From the carefully-structured records of these interviews, Lazarsfeld and his partners were able to reconstruct how the people of Erie County decided between Franklin Roosevelt and Wendell Willkie. Their results were published four years later in a book called *The People's Choice* — a little monograph that dramatically changed social scientists' perspective on the media.

The Lazarsfeld group divided the potential political effects of the press into three categories. First, they argued, the media could serve to *activate* voters in the campaign — that is, to arouse public interest and encourage voters to seek out information about candidates and issues. Second, campaign press coverage could *reinforce* existing political beliefs and bolster against change. Finally, campaign "propaganda" — as these authors called it — could *convert* voters from one candidate or party to another.

There was ample evidence in Erie County of activation by the media. People who read or listened to a substantial amount of campaign press coverage were more likely to become interested in the race. Moreover, the relationship seemed to be circular: voters exposed to a great deal of campaign coverage became more interested in the campaign, which spurred even more media use, which further heightened interest in the campaign, and so on (Lazarsfeld et al., 1944: 75-76).

But Lazarsfeld and his associates found that activation was selective. As people became interested in the campaign and decided to read or listen to more about it, they tended to seek out stories *which were consistent with their prior political attitudes.* In other words, Democrats were inclined to look for stories which spoke favorably of Roosevelt or Roosevelt's policies, while Republicans were inclined to select stories favorable to Willkie. This property of *selective attention,* the Lazarsfeld group argued, "thus *reinforces* the predispositions with which (the voter) comes to the campaign.... Whatever the publicity that is put out, it is the selective attention of the citizen which determines what is responded to" *(Ibid.:* 76, emphasis added).

Lazarsfeld, Berelson, and Gaudet attributed selective attention to two factors:

One is external to the voter himself. He lives in the country so he reads farm journals that happen also to be more Republican; or he lives in the city so he hears more talk from fellow-workers who are pro-labor and pro-Democratic. *The environment sifts the propaganda which the respondent sees and hears.* But there is also an effect caused by the still-unconscious psychological predispositions of the voter himself. From his many past experiences shared with others in his economic, religious, and community groups, he has a readiness to attend to some things more than others. His internal as well as his external situation is weighted one way or the other. Voters somehow contrive to select out of the passing stream of stimuli those by which they are more inclined to be persuaded. So it is that *the more they read and listen, the more convinced they become of the rightness of their own position. (Ibid.:* 81-82, emphasis added)

Articles and commentary in the press did convert some people in Erie County. Republicans exposed to Democratic newspapers were 32 percent more likely to vote for Roosevelt than Republicans who only read GOP papers; Democrats who read Republican newspapers were 24 percent more likely to vote for Willkie. Still, Roosevelt received 64 percent of the Democratic vote, and Willkie garnered 75 percent of the Republican vote *(Ibid.:* 96).

Among voters predisposed for one candidate or the other, then, the primary impact of the press was to reinforce rather than to convert. But what of those voters without strong predispositions? Such voters might have been more receptive to campaign propaganda — but it never reached them. According to the Lazarsfeld report, "the people who were most open to conversion — the ones the campaign managers most wanted to reach — read and listened least" *(Ibid.:* 95).

Consequently, if the press contributed to conversion, in most cases it did so *indirectly*, by altering the beliefs of those highly-activated, highly-informed people whom others looked to for opinions and political advice. About one-fifth of the Erie County residents interviewed by the Lazarsfeld team said they had either tried recently to convince someone of their political ideas or had been asked for advice on a political question. These "opinion leaders" were more likely to be interested in the election, more likely to talk about politics with friends, more likely to read or listen to the media, and more likely to report obtaining political information from the media than from personal relationships. Lazarsfeld and his associates concluded that mass communication works in two steps: ideas first move from the media to opinion leaders, and then from opinion leaders to less-active citizens *(Ibid.:* 49-51, 151).

This suggested that the media's potential for affecting elections was very different than the prevailing folklore. Generally, the Erie County experience indicated, *the media served to reinforce the status quo, not to alter it.* Where the media did spark significant attitudinal change, such change usually required the interpersonal support of opinion leaders. Compared to other social institutions, the press seemed to be rather a weakling. Lazarsfeld and another Columbia sociologist, Robert K. Merton, put it this way:

> It is our tentative judgment that the social role played by the very existence of the mass media has been commonly overestimated. . . . It is not unlikely that the invention of the automobile and its development into a mass-owned commodity has had a significantly greater effect upon society than the invention of the radio and its development into a medium of mass communication. Consider the social complexes into which the automobile has entered. Its sheer existence has exerted pressure for vastly improved roads, and, with these, mobility has increased enormously. The shape of metropolitan agglomerations has been significantly affected by the automobile. And, it may be submitted, the inventions which enlarge the radius of movement and action exert a greater influence upon social outlook and daily routines than inventions which provide avenues for ideas — ideas which can be avoided by withdrawal, deflected by resistance, and transformed by assimilation. (Lazarsfeld and Merton, 1971: 558-559)

Other research supported the Erie County findings. Lazarsfeld, Berelson, and William McPhee staged another single-locale study eight years later in Elmira, New York (Berelson et al., 1954). The Elmira results basically duplicated what had been encountered in Erie County — campaign press coverage converted very few voters from Truman to Dewey or vice versa; information and ideas seemed to be disseminated in a "two-step flow."

The first nationwide study of the media's impact on elections came in 1952, when the University of Michigan's Survey Research Center launched its series of intensive biennial polls. It was a propitious year to begin: the 1952 Eisenhower-Stevenson race was the first to be covered by network television. But neither the new medium nor the old ones seemed to make much difference. Michigan's Angus Campbell, Gerald Gurin, and Warren E. Miller found that citizens who depended on television for most of their information about the campaign were just as likely to vote for Eisenhower as those who depended upon radio or newspapers (Campbell et al., 1953: 47-48). The Stevenson vote did vary somewhat, and magazine readers were significantly more likely to vote for Eisenhower, but geographic and social factors, rather than media exposure, appeared to be the cause.

By the mid-'50s, then, social scientists appeared to have come up with an answer for one of the most important questions in modern politics: does the press influence elections? "Not really," the data said. Yet somehow that answer seemed too clean, too simple. Moreover, the media themselves were undergoing dramatic changes. When the dust settled, social scientists looked again, — and this time found some different answers.

3. From Milquetoast to. . . ?

One might say that television news came of age September 2, 1963. On that evening, CBS inaugurated the first daily half-hour newscast on network television. It was the seed of a movement that would drastically modify the character of political information commonly available in American society.

Television news in the '50s was generally a sorry affair. There were high points now and again: the *See It Now* documentaries of Edward R. Murrow and Fred Friendly on CBS; NBC's inspired pairing of Chet Huntley and David Brinkley. But the prevalent industry attitude — especially among the managements of local stations — was that news was an inconvenience whose presence on the air had to be endured because the federal government's licensing rules required it*. News didn't matter because news didn't make money; indeed, at the network level, it lost millions.

Through the '50s, the nightly network newscast was a 15-minute headline service, typically read by one man seated in front of a wall map. There were few on-the-scene reports; since video tape and satellites were still laboratory dreams, the only means for capturing events was film — which had to be flown to New York for broadcast, often with several days' delay. Local news programs were frequently dull, insipid incantations of the city newspaper's front page.

But the half-hour program was a vote of confidence that television news could be something more. It was born because network executives, reeling from a series of quiz show scandals that shook the industry around 1960, wanted to show that television could be a positive force in public life (and therefore didn't need to be regulated further by the government, as some proposed). It survived because its creators figured out that news could be visually appealing — informative, yet exciting to watch, and therefore capable of drawing an audience.

In a decade that was everywhere wild and tempestuous, television was the most revolutionary branch of journalism. Its transformation from "talking heads" to talking international drama transformed all of American newsgathering — and all of those social scientists who studied it. Television's astonishing ability to capture an audience for news — millions upon millions watching, live, the funeral of John Kennedy and the assassination of his alleged killer, watching demonstrations and urban riots, watching war in Vietnam — prompted mass communication researchers to go back and look again.

Some made new discoveries in old evidence — the Eisenhower-era University of Michigan national election studies. V.O. Key reported that frequent media users were more likely to support free enterprise and to oppose isolationist foreign policy, even after allowing for differences in education as a factor (1961: 399-401). Philip Converse demonstrated that uninvolved voters are susceptible to conversion if any new information reaches them (1962).

Others considered new evidence. Bradley S. Greenberg showed that large audiences can glean information directly from the media without the intercession of an opinion leader — that is, that mass communication doesn't necessarily work in a "two-step flow" (1964). More than three-fourths of Americans learned about President Kennedy's death from the media, Greenberg reported. Less than 25 percent heard of the shooting from personal sources.

Two articles by John Robinson (1972, 1974) considered the effect of newspaper endorsements on voting in presidential elections. Working with data

*In order to reduce interference, access to the airwaves is limited by federal regulations. Station owners are required to demonstrate to the Federal Communications Commission that they serve the "public interest, convenience, and necessity." Ordinarily, the FCC considers a certain amount of news programming a necessity.

from five University of Michigan national surveys, Robinson determined that independents — voters without party loyalties — seemed most susceptible to influence from endorsements. Independents who read newspapers which endorsed the Democratic candidate were as much as 35 percent more likely to vote Democratic than those who read Republican newspapers. The effect of endorsements on partisans, however, was erratic. Partisans appeared to be swayed by editorials only in "landslide" elections, such as the Johnson-Goldwater and Nixon-McGovern contests (1974: 592-593).

The initial signs that television might not be as benign as the '50s researchers had thought came in a study of the 1964 British parliamentary election by Jay G. Blumler and Denis McQuail (1969). Blumler and McQuail interviewed 750 voters in two northern England constituencies before and after the election campaign. They discovered that regular viewers of television news developed significantly different perceptions of the Liberal and Conservative parties. The television news audience rated the Liberals much more favorably than non-viewers, and was less likely to be critical of Conservative Prime Minister Alec Douglas-Home. There was little difference, however, between viewers and non-viewers regarding the Labour Party, which won the election.

Clearly the mass media did more than reinforce the status quo. At the very least, they helped define just what the status quo was. The media might not be able to dominate politics, but the new data indicated that they greatly determined which issues were addressed by the political system. The press "may not be successful much of the time in telling people what to think," wrote Bernard Cohen, "but it is stunningly successful in telling people what to think *about*. . . . The editor may believe he is only printing the things that people want to read, but he is thereby putting a claim on their attention, powerfully determining what they will be thinking about, and talking about, until the next wave laps their shore" (1963: 13).

This *agenda-setting* function of the press has been a major subject of mass communication research — perhaps the number one research subject — for the past 20 years. For if the press could be shown to wield substantial control over the political agenda, as Cohen conjectured, its influence on politics might not have been overestimated after all. Investigators realized that manipulating the agenda of politics can reach the same end as dictating decisions outright: it simply makes it appear as if there never was a choice to be made.

The power of the press to set the agenda for voters in a presidential campaign was explored by Maxwell McCombs and Donald Shaw (1972) during the 1968 race between Nixon, Humphrey, and Wallace. Prior to the election, McCombs and Shaw conducted 100 interviews in five "representative" precincts in Chapel Hill, North Carolina. Only voters who hadn't yet decided between candidates were interviewed, on the presumption that these individuals would be the most receptive to campaign information.

McCombs and Shaw compared what voters said were the key issues in the campaign with the amount of space devoted to those issues in the media voters used. They found "a very strong relationship between the emphasis placed on different campaign issues by the media...and the judgments of voters as to the salience and importance of various campaign topics" *(Ibid.:* 180-181).

A national study extending over several years reached similar conclusions. For the period 1964 to 1970, G. Ray Funkhouser compared what Americans identified as the most important problem facing the nation, according to the Gallup Poll, with listings of newsmagazine content in the *Readers' Guide*. He found that the agendas espoused by voters and the media were much alike, but that the salience of issues differed. "The amount of coverage in the media apparently is strongly related to the *general importance* of issues in the public's estimation," Funkhouser reported, "but less so to the public's attitudes regarding the issues or their priorities in dealing with them" (1973: 71, emphasis in original)*.

Most journalists believe that if the press does set the political agenda, it does so in an unbiased, "objective" manner that accurately reflects the conflicts facing society. Indeed, the metaphor they use most often is a mirror which reproduces exactly what it sees. Frank Stanton, then president of CBS, told a 1968 congressional hearing: "What the media do is to hold a mirror up to society and try to report it as faithfully as possible" (quoted in Epstein, 1973: 13-14).

But there are ample indications that the media's mirror, like those in carnival fun houses, distorts as it reflects. Very few scholars believe this distortion results from a conscious conspiracy by the media to deceive the public**. Rather, they believe it is the unconscious yet inevitable result of the media's operating practices and of journalists' personal values.

Much as any other organizations, newspapers, magazines, and network news divisions devise standard routines for getting their work done adequately and on time. Events that coincide with these routines are more likely to be picked up as news (cf. Epstein, 1973; Sigal, 1973; Blomquist, 1979; Gans, 1979).

The work day of most city government reporters, for example, begins with a walk through city hall, stopping at each office to ask "what's new." This insures that no major city decision will be overlooked. However, since the reporter is looking first to city officials for story ideas, the articles appearing

*Neither of these studies is ideal. The decision of McCombs and Shaw to limit their research to undecided voters is troubling; one would like to know how the media compares with other agenda cues, such as party identification, which are likely to be stronger in voters who decide early on. Funkhouser's reliance on the *Readers' Guide* to measure content makes no allowance for writing style or prominence of display, and doesn't take into account differences in subject preference between the newsmagazines and other media (cf. Gans, 1979: ch. 1). The greatest uncertainty, of course, is the unresolved chicken-or-the-egg question of whether the media lead voters' preferences or voters' preferences lead the media. This is how McCombs and Shaw explain their view:

> Any argument that the correlations between media and voter emphasis are spurious — that they are simply responding to the same events and not influencing each other one way or the other — assumes that voters have alternative means of observing the day-to-day changes in the political arena. This assumption is not plausible; since few directly participate in presidential election campaigns, and fewer still see presidential candidates in person, . . . mass media provide the best — and only — easily available approximation of ever-changing political realities. (1972: 185)

**For a provocative exception, see Schiller, 1973.

from his or her beat will inevitably reflect the official view of affairs more than if the work day started with, say, a tour of neighborhood groups.

Moreover, journalists tend to come from certain backgrounds and hold (or assimilate) certain ideals. Most reporters and editors are solidly middle-class — or more precisely, middle-class white males (though the racial and sexual barriers are coming down). Most were attracted to journalism by the excitement of reporting and the possibility to "do good." Most are skeptical about the motivations of government, and are especially suspicious of politicians. Yet the typical journalist is romantically optimistic about the generosity and good nature of individual citizens. Generally speaking, newspeople are, in a word, populists.

Herbert Gans (1979) contends that these populist beliefs pervade what gets selected as news. Elected officials are chastized by the press when they do not serve the public interest selflessly; capitalism is lauded but expected to be altruistic; social and moral disorder is considered dangerous and unproductive; strong, competent leadership is demanded and applauded. Drawn together, Gans asserts, these "enduring values" constitute a conservative ideology which — because it favors the middle and upper classes — inhibits a truly democratic flow of information.

Some researchers believe that the media's agenda-setting influence has been so pernicious that it has caused disruptive shifts in the value structure underlying American politics. Michael J. Robinson claims that television news has been especially harmful to political efficacy — to voters' feelings that they have a say in government. "Without discounting the importance of Vietnam, urban insurrection, and presidential assassination," writes Robinson, "I would argue that the television news system helped to foster and to amplify the changes in our political culture — changes such as the increasing levels of cynicism, pessimism, alienation, and estrangement; the increasing concern with law and order, and the 'social issue'; and the growing fascination with 'backlash' politics" (1977: 27).

Robinson offers findings of the University of Michigan's 1968 national election study as evidence of this "videomalaise." White men and women who depended entirely on television for political information were, he notes, less likely to trust other people, more likely to believe that the civil rights movement was proceeding too quickly, and more likely to vote for Nixon or Wallace — regardless of income or education (1976: 420-423).

What is it about television news that evokes "videomalaise"? Robinson maintains that television journalism is *anti-institutional* — that it emphasizes conflict, violence, and the negative aspects of events, thereby encouraging dissatisfaction with the status quo. He states: "It seems reasonable to assume that these anti-institutional themes reach the audience with one essential message: none of our national policies work, none of our institutions respond, none of our political organizations succeed" (1976: 429). Viewers absorb this dissatisfaction over time, he argues, because they believe what television tells them more than they believe any other information source.

But television has done more than incite alienation, Robinson declares. By providing candidates with a vehicle to reach voters directly, it has "denied the parties their most important function — the right to recruit and campaign for office-seekers" (1977: 20). Robinson and other observers fear that atrophy of the parties will decrease the stability of American politics, since the system will be more susceptible to abrupt changes in attitudes and support.

The current state of mass communication research, then, does not make for a neat summary. While there still are no signs that the media evoke massive changes in political behavior, it is clear that they do alter some attitudes, and the potential exists that these effects could be responsible for significant political change. In other words, there is sufficient cause for us to believe that in the right circumstances, given the right combination of message and audiences, the press can have substantial impact on electoral results.

And even if the media had negligible effect on voting and elections, it still would be important for political scientists to study them. For the old myth of the all-powerful press yet persists among politicians and other government leaders; regardless of what difference the press actually makes, politicians still behave as if it is crucial to electoral success. That alone is reason enough to take it seriously.

II. An introduction to empirical research

The immediate objective of this SETUPS is to acquaint you with some of the mass media's influences on political behavior. But there are two other important objectives here. First, we want to give you a sense of how political scientists design and carry out empirical research. Exercises in the chapter which follows will show you how to construct empirical research questions and use a sample survey to answer them. Second, and perhaps most important, we want to help you improve your ability to write about issues in political science by providing "hands-on" experience in drafting research reports.

The preceding chapter introduced you to political roles of the media. The latter two objectives are the subject of this chapter.

1. What is empirical research?

A political scientist's most valuable research tools are his or her powers of observation — the ability to discern what people are doing, saying, thinking, or feeling. Empirical research is knowledge about politics based on direct observations of the political process.

Until about 50 years ago, empirical research on the political thinking of an entire nation was all but impossible. Virtually the only directly observable events which conveyed citizens' political sentiments were elections — which, for all their democratic virtues, were imperfect measures of public opinion. Election returns were incomplete: not everyone was eligible to vote, and not all those who were eligible bothered to cast ballots. And while vote totals told who won, they couldn't say why.

In the 1930s, political scientists, sociologists, and statisticians introduced a new technique for measuring public opinion directly: the sample survey, or opinion poll. Polling permitted social scientists to go beyond the highlights of the public's political attitudes and inquire just what and how people thought about their government.

Surveys were made possible by a series of statistical discoveries around the turn of the century*. Mathematicians studying theories of chance found that

*For a more complete history of survey research, see Warwick and Lininger, 1975: ch. 1.

public opinion in a political unit of *any size* could be reliably estimated from interviews with only 1000 people — if that 1000-person sample was selected randomly; that is, by lottery.

The need for randomness in the selection of interviewees — or *respondents*, as survey researchers call them — wasn't startling. Several newspapers and magazines tried to stage "straw votes" as circulation gimmicks in the years before polling was perfected, only to find their results clouded by systematic bias in the sample. Some asked readers to send back coupons indicating their presidential choice. This method was easy prey for organized campaigns on behalf of one or another contender. Others, most notably the *Literary Digest*, pulled names from telephone directories. Unfortunately, a half-century ago telephones were the province of the better-off, and thus the *Literary Digest* sample was biased against poor people — causing it to miss the Roosevelt avalanche in 1936.

Many people, however, couldn't believe that opinion patterns for the whole country could be discerned from just 1000 interviews. Even today, with polls an accepted part of American political campaigns, many remain skeptical about survey estimates of public opinion.

It is true that surveys cannot *exactly* gauge public opinion from a relative handful of interviews. But they can come very close to the mark. The logic depends upon principles of probability — the laws which dictate, for example, that flipping a coin yields heads half the time, tails half the time.

In practice, of course, coin flipping rarely works out that way: flip a coin a hundred times and almost always, purely by chance, you will wind up with either more heads than tails or the other way around. Nevertheless, the variation from 50-50 is predictable. Odds are about three to one that the number of heads will be between 45 and 55, and about 100 to one that it will be between 37 and 63.

What works for predicting coins also works for approximating public opinion. Suppose that someone managed to interview every adult American about a certain issue, and found that 70 percent supported the President's stand and 30 percent opposed it. Odds are only about one in 20 that interviews with 1000 people would differ by more than four percent from the values obtained by questioning everyone. This accuracy range is called the *confidence interval*.

Surveys are bound to contain some additional error beyond these purely statistical differences. As in the *Literary Digest* example, an ostensibly random sample may turn out to contain biases. (Some compromises on randomness are almost always inevitable; a perfectly random sample is ordinarily too costly to be practicable.) Questions may be so densely phrased that respondents cannot understand them, or be put so loosely that the answers are meaningless. Interviewers may fail to establish rapport with respondents, making them reluctant to reveal their true feelings. Yet with careful planning, the impact of these non-statistical pitfalls can be kept to a minimum.

The survey we will be using in this SETUPS, the 1980 National Election Study (NES), reflects the most careful planning possible. It was administered by a team of social scientists based at the University of Michigan's Center for Political

Studies and Institute for Social Research — arguably the best survey organizations in the nation. For the sections of the NES we will analyze, slightly more than 1400 men and women were interviewed before and after the 1980 presidential election.

The NES differs from the election-time polls conducted by newspapers and broadcast networks, though it asks many of the same questions. First, the NES is far more comprehensive. Each interview lasted on the average better than an hour, and included several hundred questions. All of the interviews were completed in person, rather than over the telephone, which permitted the interviewers to ask more complicated questions. Second, the NES wasn't conducted with the haste necessary to meet journalists' deadlines. While a Gallup or AP-NBC poll may be gathered and tabulated in a few days, the NES staff spent nearly six months reviewing interviewers' notes. Finally, unlike the typical journalism poll, the NES isn't obsessed with the single question "Who's winning?" It is intended to offer a broader picture of American politics — one that encompasses "why" and "how" as well as "who."

The Michigan group employs about 100 interviewers scattered across the country. Each is provided detailed instructions about whom to contact for interviews — instructions devised by an elaborate random selection procedure*. As notes from interviews are returned to Ann Arbor, the NES staff groups the answers to each question into categories and assigns each category a number. For example, respondents might be assigned the number one if they voted for Ronald Reagan, two if for Jimmy Carter, three if for John Anderson, four if for some other candidate, and five if they didn't vote at all. The process of converting verbal answers to numeric values is called *coding*, and the numeric representations of answers are called *variables*.

Once all the interviews have been coded, the variables are entered into a computer so they can be counted automatically. The format of a survey as it has been stored in the computer is described in a *codebook*. Appendix A contains the codebook for those parts of the NES we will use in this SETUPS. It shows how questions were broken into variables for coding, the computer "name" given to each variable, the categories that were created for answers and the numbers assigned to each, and the number of respondents put into each category. Here is a sample entry, for respondent's level of education:

EDUC   R'S EDUCATION (V486)   DK 1, COL 11

        Highest level of education attained by R.

        344 1. Less than high school degree
        515 2. High school degree
        545 3. Some college
          4 9. DK or NA

*Our discussion of survey research methods and statistics here is necessarily brief. Warwick and Lininger (1975) or Weisberg and Bowen (1979) provide excellent detailed explanations.

"EDUC" is the name given this variable inside the computer. The phrase "R's education" is a brief description of the variable ("R" is a common survey abbreviation for "respondent"). The number following this phrase indicates that EDUC was the 486th variable in the original version prepared by the Center for Political Studies*. The phrase "DK 1, COL 11" tells where EDUC can be found in the computer's record of the survey (your instructor will describe how to use this information). The next block of text contains either the question, exactly as put to respondents, or a note explaining the variable. It is followed by a line for each category. The first number tells how many respondents were placed in that category. This number is often referred to as the *marginal*. The second number is the value assigned to the category. The last entry states what the category includes. For example, the first category for respondent's education contains 344 respondents, carries the value one, and includes respondents who completed less than 12 years of school (i.e. didn't finish high school). The sum of all the marginals for an item should always equal the sample size — in this case, 1408.

One could start research just with information from the codebook — no computer necessary. From the marginals in the example above, for instance, we can find out how well educated Americans are. We observe that about three-quarters of our sample finished high school ((515 +545)/1408); 39 percent (545/1408) completed some college. As an exercise, verify from the codebook that television is the most important source of political information for 54 percent of our sample (variable MOSTIMP, page 61).

Though these marginal results may be interesting, they aren't satisfying — at least not to the political scientist, who wants to learn not just *what* happens in politics, but *why* it happens. The codebook can tell us that most people turn first to television for political news, but it alone cannot tell us why television is the majority's first choice — or how that preference affects election outcomes. For that, we need to look for relationships *between* variables.

Two variables are said to be related if the values of one tend to be predictable from the values of the other. Consider the case of education and income. Generally speaking, better-educated people make more money; education and income are related. Moreover, since as education increases, income tends to increase as well, we can say they are *positively* related; that is, they change in the same direction. If one variable got larger when the other got smaller — as for, say, education and unemployment —, we would say they were *negatively* or *inversely* related.

Just because two variables are related does not mean that one causes the other. Coincidence produces many curious statistical relationships. In one well-known instance, the English statisticians G. Udny Yule and M.G. Kendall found that the percentage of Britons judged mentally defective between 1924 and 1937 was positively related — almost perfectly — to the number of radios in use during the period (1950: 315-316). Yet no one would suggest that radio causes mental defects. The relationship is merely a bizarre artifact.

*For details, see the codebook.

Therefore, before you can claim that a statistical relationship has any substantive significance, you must first develop a plausible scenario of cause and effect. In other words, the *first* step in conducting empirical research is *construction of a hypothesis* — an educated guess, based on your readings, of how things work and why.

Your hypothesis should be as clear as you can make it, since your statistical research will be a test of it. For example, you would be asking for trouble with the hypothesis: "Education and income are related." So how are they related? Why do you think they are related that way? Which variable is the cause, or *independent variable*, and which the effect, or *dependent variable**? *What are you looking for and why do you expect to find it?* A better hypothesis would be: "People with more education are likely to have skills which qualify them for more complicated, specialized careers. Since specialized jobs generally pay more, people with more education are likely to make more money."

Statisticians offer us a variety of techniques for testing hypotheses. This SETUPS will use the most common one: *contingency table analysis*, also called *crosstabulation*.

2. Contingency table analysis — two variables

The simplest means for examining relationships between variables is a *contingency table*. Contingency tables contain one column for each value of the independent variable and one row for each value of the dependent variable (ordinarily omitting "don't know" and "no answer" responses, which are declared *missing* and excluded). The intersection of these rows and columns covers every possible combination (i.e., every possible *contingency*) of the two variables. Either by hand or with a computer, the number of respondents with each combination is determined and recorded at the corresponding place, or *cell*, in the table.

Suppose we wanted to test this hypothesis: "Better-educated people are likely to be more inquisitve about public affairs than people with minimal education, since education encourages seeking out answers to questions. Therefore, better-educated people will tend to use more media to get campaign information." We use the computer to generate a six-cell table with number of media used to obtain campaign information (MEDIAUSE) as the dependent variable and education (EDUC) as the independent variable (table 1).

We read the table this way: of those survey respondents who completed 11 years or less of school, 242 used two or less media to get information about the 1980 campaign, while 102 used three or four media. Among those respondents who finished at least a year of college, 181 used two or less media, but 364 used three or four media. Our hypothesis is confirmed. Respondents with more schooling tended to use more media.

Notice that the table totes up the number of cases in each column and the

---

*An easy way to remember which is which: the *dependent* variable, the effect, *depends* upon the independent variable, the cause.

Table 1. Media use by level of education

NUMBER OF MEDIA USED TO OBTAIN INFORMATION	EDUCATION		
	0-11 grades	High school	Some college
0-2	242	302	181
3-4	102	213	364
	344	515	545

1404 = table total
4 missing cases
1408 = sample size

Source: 1980 National Election Study

number of missing cases. This permits statistically-minded readers to compute confidence intervals for your findings. It also is considered good form to cite with the table the source of the data being analyzed.

Tables are much easier to understand with the clumsy cell totals converted to percentages, as in table 2.

Table 2. Media use by level of education (percentaged)

NUMBER OF MEDIA USED TO OBTAIN INFORMATION	EDUCATION		
	0-11 grades	High school	Some college
0-2	70%	59%	33%
3-4	30	41	67
	100%	100%	100%
N =	344	515	545

1404 = table total
4 missing cases
1408 = sample size

Source: 1980 National Election Study

Armed with percentages, we can describe the relationship between media use and education plainly yet precisely. We observe, for instance, that respondents with some college were 37 percent more likely to use three or four media than those who didn't graduate from high school (67 − 30 = 37).

Percentages are always calculated to add up to 100 for each value of the independent variable, which usually appears across the top of the table (probably because we are accustomed to summing figures down rather than across). Again, the number of respondents in each column (the N) is supplied to permit derivation of confidence intervals.

How can we tell whether a percentage difference represents a real discrepancy between categories of respondents or just sampling error? Well, we never can be certain; remember that there is bound to be some chance of inaccuracy in every survey statistic. There is, however, an accepted dividing line. We can compute a confidence interval which corrects percentages for 95 out of every 100 cases of sampling error. If the difference between two percentages is larger than that interval, we say it is *statistically significant* with 95 percent confidence. That is, we accept the chance of making a mistake five percent of the time. But if the percentage difference is less than that interval, we chalk it up to chance and say there is *no significant difference* between categories.

The formula for computing the 95 percent confidence interval of a percentage difference is

$$\pm 1.96 \sqrt{\frac{(p_1)(1-p_1)}{n_1} + \frac{(p_2)(1-p_2)}{n_2}},$$

where p_1 and p_2 are the two percentages, expressed as fractions of one (i.e. 20 percent = .20), and where n_1 and n_2 are the numbers of respondents in the columns from which the percentages are drawn*. For example, consider once more the finding from the table above that respondents with some college were 37 percent more likely to use three or four media than respondents without a high school diploma. The 95 percent confidence interval for this difference is

$$\pm 1.96 \sqrt{\frac{(.30)(1-.30)}{344} + \frac{(.67)(1-.67)}{545}} = \pm 0.062,$$

or about six percent in either direction. Since this is much less than the difference we found, we can say our results are statistically significant with at least 95 percent confidence. Alternatively, we can say that highly-educated people were 37 percent more likely than minimally-educated people, plus or minus six percent, to use three or four media.

Another means for checking whether differences in a table are statistically significant or the product of sampling error is the *chi-square test*. Instead of working two cells at a time, chi-square determines if the distribution of cases throughout an entire table is significantly different from chance**. Most computer programs used for survey analysis will calculate chi-square for you.

To meet the 95-percent confidence requirement, chi-square must be greater than or equal to a key value, which varies with a measure of the number of cells in the table. This measure, called *degrees of freedom* (abbreviated *df*), is equal to the number of rows in the table minus one times the number of columns in the table minus one. In the table above, chi-square = 132.44 with two degrees of freedom ((3 − 1) × (2 − 1)). For two degrees of freedom, as a chart in any statistics text will attest, chi-square must be greater than or equal to 5.99 to meet the 95-percent confidence requirement. Since chi-square ex-

*Derived from Taylor et al., 1976: 41. These authors would further recommend multiplying n_1 and n_2 by .67 as an adjustment for deviations from randomness necessary in devising practical national samples.

**Be aware, however, that a table found significant overall by chi-square can contain insignificant percentage differences. One test doesn't substutite for the other; you must perform both to be certain.

ceeds that level in this table, we can say that the positive relationship we report between media use and education is statistically significant at the 95-percent level, according to the chi-square test.

In addition to tests for sampling error, some data analysis programs will also compute useful numbers called *summary statistics*. These indexes of the direction and strength of relationships are very convenient for comparing findings from several tables.

One widely-used summary statistic is named *gamma*. It is appropriate for describing any relationship where the values of both the independent and dependent variables form scales with a logical order. MEDIAUSE and EDUC meet these terms: the values of MEDIAUSE denote increasing levels of media use; the value of EDUC denote increasing levels of education. But the variable MOSTIMP, the respondent's most important source of campaign information, does not: it consists of arbitrary categories with no rational ranking. Gamma could not be used, then, to summarize a relationship involving MOSTIMP.

Gamma varies between −1 and 1. A negative relationship between two variables yields a negative value for gamma; a positive relationship yields a positive gamma. The strength of the relationship is indicated by gamma's absolute value. Nearly-perfect relationships have gammas close to −1 or 1; unrelated variables have a gamma of zero.

In practice, it takes some experience to concoct meaningful interpretations for gamma. In the table above, for example, gamma = +.48. Just what does that mean? It signifies a positive relationship, to be sure, but does it suggest we've found a particularly strong positive relationship? Here are some conventions for converting gamma into words*:

VALUE OF GAMMA	APPROPRIATE PHRASE
+.50 or higher	A very strong positive relationship
+.36 to +.49	A substantial positive relationship
+.20 to +.35	A moderate positive relationship
+.10 to +.19	A low positive relationship
+.01 to +.09	A negligible positive relationship
.00	No relationship
−.01 to −.09	A negligible negative relationship
−.10 to −.19	A low negative relationship
−.20 to −.35	A moderate negative relationship
−.36 to −.49	A substantial negative relationship
−.50 or lower	A very strong negative relationship

3. Contingency table analysis — many variables

Empirical research generally begins with two-variable hypotheses. Yet few political effects can be attributed to a single cause. Therefore, once we have

*This table is inspired by a similar one for the summary statistic Yule's Q in Davis, 1971, p. 49.

established the relationship between two variables, we usually expand our research to ascertain how other variables affect that relationship.

Suppose, for example, we had tested the hypothesis that people who use the media intensively (variable INTENSE) tend to be better informed about politics (variable INFO), producing the results shown in table 3.

Table 3. Level of campaign information by intensity of media use

INTENSITY OF MEDIA USE

CAMPAIGN INFORMATION LEVEL	Very Low/ Low	High/ Very High	
Poorly informed	58%	25%	
Moderately informed	27	31	
Well informed	15	44	
	100%	100%	
N =	701	707	1408 = table total
			1408 = sample size

Chi-square = 190.44 with 2 df
(significant at better than 95% confidence level)

Gamma = 0.56

Source: 1980 National Election Study

On paper, our hypothesis has been confirmed: high-intensity media users were 29 percent more likely than low-intensity users to be well informed. Yet we know that both political information and media use are also positively related to education. How can we be certain that the correlation observed here is attributable to media exposure, and not because high-intensity media users are likely to be well-educated?

The solution is to break this table into three smaller tables, identical in format, but with each containing respondents from just one of our three educational groupings. If the significant difference observed above disappears with education held constant, or *controlled*, then we will conclude that education — not intensity of media use — explains political information. On the other hand, if the smaller tables still show a significant difference between low-intensity and high-intensity media users, we will know education isn't to blame.

Table 4 shows the results.

The original hypothesis holds: even with education controlled, intensive media users were more likely than infrequent users to be informed about politics. But the relationship is not uniform; media exposure does not have the same impact on all educational groups. Among respondents who completed some college, high-intensity media users were 34 percent more likely than low-intensity users to be well informed. Among high school graduates, however,

Table 4. Level of campaign information by education and intensity of media use

EDUCATION AND INTENSITY OF MEDIA USE

	0-11 grades		High school		Some college	
	Very Low/Low	High/Very High	Very Low/Low	High/Very High	Very Low/Low	High/Very High
CAMPAIGN INFORMATION LEVEL						
Poorly informed	76%	54%	58%	31%	36%	11%
Moderately informed	15	27	29	36	37	28
Well informed	9	19	13	33	27	61
	100%	100%	100%	100%	100%	100%
N =	211	133	302	213	187	358

1404 = table total
4 missing cases
1408 = sample size

For 0-11 grades
Chi-square = 18.45 with 2 df
(significant at better than 95% confidence level)
Gamma = 0.42

For high school
Chi-square = 45.25 with 2 df
(significant at better than 95% confidence level)
Gamma = 0.48

For some college
Chi-square = 73.78 with 2 df
(significant at better than 95% confidence level)
Gamma = 0.58

Source: 1980 National Election Study

high-intensity users were only 20 percent more likely to be well informed. And among respondents without a high school diploma, the difference was 10 percent. This is termed an *interaction effect,* with education *specifying* the relationship between intensity of media use and information.

Although we have demonstrated that media use affects political knowledge independent of education, we shouldn't overlook the message in this table that education is by far the more potent influence. This can be seen by computing percentage differences between the subtables. Notice, for instance, that high-intensity media users with some college were 28 percent more likely to be well informed than high-intensity users who only completed high school, and 42 percent more likely to be well informed than high-intensity users without a high school diploma.

The logic of contingency table analysis can be extended in this way to as many variables as the researcher wishes — with one handicap. As the number of subtables created by adding control variables increases, the average number of respondents in each subtable column decreases. As that happens, confidence intervals grow larger, quickly reaching the point where nothing short of a statistical tidal wave can be proven significant. (The confidence intervals for our three-variable example above are between 10 and 13 percent.) Four variables is ordinarily the limit for a survey of 1500 respondents — and even that is pushing things much of the time. Moreover, on a practical level, hypotheses with more than three or four variables usually are so awkward that they are impossible to talk about in plain English.

Before tacking on more variables, then, always ask: *Will these variables explain substantially more than what my hypothesis already includes?* Simplicity, not complexity, makes for quality empirical research.

4. Writing the research report

There is no such thing as *the* perfect research report. There are papers which answer, plainly yet explicitly, all the questions about their subject that fill a reader's mind. There are papers which capture the essence of their subject so powerfully that they suggest new issues, new consequences. Yet for any subject, there can be a dozen such papers — all choosing different routes, yet equally effective.

Still, all good papers share some traits. For regardless of approach, form, or style, all argumentative prose has the same intent: to tell other people what you think about your subject and why you think that way. That means all argumentative prose follows, in some fashion, the same agenda. It looks something like this:

1) *What is the research question here?* Before doing much else, an essay needs to establish a starting point. Just what are you going to discuss? If your subject is a subdivision of some larger question, how big a bite will you take?

2) *What are the possible answers to that question?* The meat of any paper is conflict; after all, if there isn't more than one answer to a research question, the exercise is trivial. So next an essay should introduce the reader to that

conflict, making explicit references to articles and/or books supporting each view.

3) What do you think is the best answer? How will you prove that? With the issue and conflict set down, the reader then needs a goal to look toward, and a road map of how you plan to get there. Early on, then, a paper should state concisely your assessment of the situation — your hypothesis — and how you will show that this assessment fits the facts better than others. When using surveys, you should describe the data you will use — how and by whom it was collected; what relevant questions were asked; how you will define variables for analysis.

4) State your case. Show, *with examples,* how the evidence supports your explanation over competing answers. Don't lose the facts in the numbers: say "better-educated people are likely to use more media," not "there is a relationship of gamma = .48 between education and media use."

5) So what? What difference does it make that your explanation holds rather than another? Why does what you've found make your research question something worth asking? What implications do your results have for future research in this field?

Obviously this format shouldn't be followed blindly. Above all in your writing, be yourself. Don't try to second-guess what the grader wants to see; second-guessing is phony and usually wrong. By the same token, however, don't force your reader to second-guess you. Be sure you say what you mean, and say it so others can understand it. A clear, simple, direct argument is worth its weight in gold — and is as close to perfect as anyone could expect.

III. Exercises

That old maxim which claims experience is the greatest teacher unquestionably applies to empirical research. The sheer mechanics of generating tables aren't difficult, once you've conquered any initial trepidation about computers*. But the process of concocting a research question, picking the right variables to test it, and interpreting the computer output demands a certain shrewdness and intuition that only comes with practice.

Practice is the purpose of this chapter. The five exercises below are actual empirical research problems, just like those we would find described in political science journals. Your task will be to find some answers.

The first exercise tells you exactly what to do to answer the question it poses; when you finish all its instructions, you will have completed your first piece of empirical research. The succeeding exercises, however, leave progressively more of the research strategy up to you. The fifth exercise provides only the questions; how and with what data to answer them will be entirely your choice. When you complete that assignment, you should be ready for the exercise that offers the best experience of all — designing your own research problem.

1. Who uses the media?

Because the media are so ubiquitous, we might assume that everyone makes substantial use of them. In some respects, that is certainly the case: the average American watches two hours of television daily and reads at least one newspaper most every day**. Nevertheless, neither the network news audience nor the newspaper audience is representative of the country as a whole.

---

*Admittedly, there *is* something intimidating about machines that demand complete perfection when you talk to them but often respond only in a queer stilted code; that label your mistakes "fatal errors"; that can tear apart a couple hours or more of your work in seconds. But remember, for all their arrogance, computers are merely supercharged calculators. And they have one very redeeming quality: they never run out of patience. You will never have a more exacting yet forgiving research partner.

**According to data in the 1977 General Social Survey conducted by the National Opinion Research Center, University of Chicago.

Network news viewers are disproportionately poor and older. According to figures cited by Herbert Gans (1979: 222), half of the adult audience for the CBS Evening News in 1974 was 55 years of age or older; better than 40 percent had household incomes under $8000. Newspaper readers, on the other hand, tend to be wealthier and better-educated. People with greater income and education also are more likely to use several media to follow politics (Key, 1961, ch. 14; Tichenor et al., 1970).

As our first research exercise, you will examine who used which media in the 1980 campaign, and to what extent.

Research questions:
1. What types of people are most frequently exposed to mass communication about politics? Consider these dependent variables: MEDIAUSE (number of media used to obtain information about the campaign) and INTENSE (intensity of campaign media exposure). Prepare two-variable tables using some or all of the following demographic items as the independent variable: AGE, SEX, RACE, INCOME, REGION (that is, the region of the country where the interview took place), EDUC (respondent's education), RELIG (religion), MARSTAT (marital status), and PARTYID (party identification). Explain your findings.
2. What groups of people depend most upon television for information about politics? What groups followed the campaign primarily through newspapers and magazines? Dependent variable: MOSTIMP (most important source of campaign information). Independent variables: demographic items listed in question 1. Explain your findings.

2. Concern for issues

In chapter 1, we argued that the media are more effective at shaping the public's policy agenda than altering specific political behaviors. The content of this agenda is fairly meaningless, however, if people are indifferent to how issues are resolved. We should test, then, whether people who are more active media users are also more likely to be concerned about the issues they believe are important.

Our respondents were asked to name the most important national problem. Then they were asked how concerned they were about this problem (variable CONCERN). Using variable INTENSE (intensity of media use) as an index of exposure to the media, the two-variable relationship is shown in table 1.

Research questions:
1. Describe the relationship between media exposure and concern for the most important national problem.
2. What control variables should be added to our analysis? Why?
3. Prepare several three-variable tables to determine the impact of controls. Explain your results. Which variable has the greater influence on concern for the most important problem, media exposure or the control? Why do you think this is so?

Table 1. Concern for most important national problem by intensity of media use

CONCERN FOR MOST IMPORTANT NATIONAL PROBLEM	INTENSITY OF MEDIA USE	
	Very Low/Low	High/Very High
Extremely concerned	43%	57%
Very concerned	42	37
Somewhat/A little	15	6
	100%	100%
N =	655	695

1350 = table total
 58 missing cases
1408 = sample size

Chi-square = 40.30 with 2 df
 (significant at 95% level)

Gamma = − 0.28

Source: 1980 National Election Study

3. Agenda-setting

As we reported in chapter 1, several studies have found strong correlations between the set of issues covered by the press and the set of problems respondents say are the most important. Did this relationship hold for the 1980 campaign?

To determine the issues which dominated press coverage, we examined copies of the *New York Times* front page and transcripts of the first three segments of the *CBS Evening News* for August and September, 1980 — the two months prior to the interview in which our respondents were asked to name the most important national problem*. Table 2 shows the results.

Research questions:

1. Compare respondents' views of the most important national problem (variable PROBLEM) with the media content reported in table 2. How are they similar?

2. Are the agendas of frequent media users more likely to resemble the media's agenda?

3. What control variables should be considered, if any? Why? What are the results?

---

*This is hardly a perfect measure of what the nation's press covered in these two months; there are often considerable differences from one newspaper or broadcast to another. A better index would also include three or four other newspapers, a newsmagazine, and the ABC and CBS newscasts.

Table 2. Subject matter of leading stories, *New York Times* and *CBS Evening News*, August-September, 1980

	New York Times	CBS News
Economy/National development	17%	19%
Social services	9	10
Public order/Morality/ Ethics in government	16	14
Foreign affairs	58	58
	100%	100%
Number of stories =	303	397

Source: Content analysis prepared by Jon Kenton of Harvard College under the author's direction.*

*Stories which reported campaign events without directly discussing issues were excluded from analysis. The *CBS Morning News* was substituted on two occasions where the *CBS Evening News* was preempted by special programming.

4. Campaign participation

An extensive study by Sidney Verba and Norman Nie (1972) found that participation in politics is related to five variables: social status, age, race, organizational membership, and partisanship. According to Verba and Nie, people who are active in politics are likely to be better-off, older, white, members of organizations, and strong partisans.

Verba and Nie didn't examine the impact of media use on participation. But in a classic article, the sociologists Paul Lazarsfeld and Robert Merton contend that exposure to the media makes people less likely to participate in politics. They explain:

> Exposure to . . . [the media] may serve to narcotize rather than to energize the average reader or listener. As an increasing meed of time is devoted to reading and listening, a decreasing share is available for organized action. The individual reads accounts of issues and problems and may even discuss alternative lines of action. But this rather intellectualized, rather remote connection with organized social action is not activated. The interested and informed citizen can congratulate himself on his lofty state of interest and information and neglect to see that he has abstained from decision and action. In short, he takes his secondary contact with the world of political reality, his reading and listening and thinking, as a vicarious performance. He comes to mistake *knowing* about problems of the day for *doing* something about them. (Lazarsfeld and Merton, 1971: 565-566, emphasis in original)

Research questions:

1. Are intensive media users more likely or less likely than infrequent users to be interested in the campaign?

2. Are media users less likely to vote? Are they less likely to participate in other ways (such as giving money to candidates or wearing a campaign button)? Explain your findings.

3. What control variables should be considered, if any? Why? What are the results?

5. Explaining the vote

These questions are left for you to develop your own hypotheses and determine the most appropriate variables for testing them.

1. Were active media users more likely to vote for one candidate or another?

2. Were active media users more likely or less likely to change their presidential preference between September and November?

3. Were readers of newspapers which endorsed Reagan more likely to vote for Reagan than readers of newspapers which endorsed Carter or Anderson?

4. Do frequent media users differ on campaign issues from infrequent users?

5. Do frequent media users perceive the candidates' personalities differently from infrequent users?

6. What was the impact of the Reagan-Carter debate?

IV. Toward a research agenda

By now you should have reached some conclusions about the media's influence on voting behavior. But you may also have found that your research raised more questions than it answered. In this final chapter, we will discuss some of these unresolved issues, and consider how political scientists might address them.

1. The press and voting behavior

We have seen in this SETUPS that frequent media users do behave somewhat differently in politics than people who aren't so heavily exposed to the media. Nevertheless, on the crucial point of whether media users vote differently than non-users, we've found that media exposure ranks well behind other variables — especially, of course, behind party identification — in explaining the election outcome. And though we saw some signs of agenda-setting, our survey evidence indicates that the press was hardly the sole determinant of this campaign's agenda.

These results shouldn't surprise us; as we saw in chapter 1, similar findings occur repeatedly throughout mass communication research. Yet they still seem incredibly counter-intuitive. It strikes one as absurd that the media could be such an integral part of a campaign, yet apparently contribute little to its outcome.

It is quite possible that our intuition simply is wrong — that, as Lazarsfeld and Merton (1971) contend, social scientists and society generally have made scapegoats of the media because they are more visible, more vulnerable to attack than other institutions. It is also possible, however, that the National Election Study data doesn't tell the whole story. The questions employed in the NES to measure media exposure and its effects have several shortcomings which limit their effectiveness. Definitive evidence of the press's impact on voting may well be slipping through the cracks.

First, with one exception, the NES only measures media use specifically related to the campaign*. It doesn't record respondents' total exposure to the

*The 1980 NES does ask respondents how often they watch network newscasts, and how much attention they pay to political news in general on television.

media: it doesn't tell us what else respondents read in newspapers and magazines, listened to on radio, and — above all — saw on television. Yet many analysts believe entertainment television — especially the situation comedies produced by Norman Lear *(All in the Family, Maude)* and Grant Tinker *(The Mary Tyler Moore Show, Rhoda)* — has been an important force for social and political change. For example, Michael J. Robinson observes:

> Between 1958 and 1969, the percentage of women accepting the idea that a woman could serve effectively as president actually *declined* by three percent. But between 1969 and 1972, the proportion of women who came to accept the idea of a female president *increased* by 19 percent. The National Organization for Women (NOW), which had been established in 1966, had had little or no effect on women's attitudes during its first three years; if anything, NOW merely provoked the development of an anti-feminist backlash among women. But during those first two seasons in which Mary Richards and Rhoda Morgenstern came to television, the level of public support for a female president increased more than during any other two-year — or 10-year — period since the 1930's. (1977:32)*

Even as a measure of campaign media usage, the NES question battery leaves something to be desired: it doesn't tell us whether the respondent saw or heard any political advertising.

Second, about the only way we can probe for media effects in the NES data is to compare frequent media users with infrequent users. In doing so, we assume that the intensity of effect increases uniformly with the intensity of media exposure — that frequent media users will be affected more than infrequent users. This premise, however, may not be tenable.

It is possible, for example, that voters who use the media less take away comparatively more from each exposure — indeed, that a single instance of media use can be as important to the voting decision as several dozen. Most voters don't come to the polling booth with detailed rationalizations for their choice (e.g. "I like Reagan because he is a fiscal conservative"); rather, they can explain their vote only in vague, oblique terms (e.g. "Reagan seems like a very smart man")(Campbell et al., 1964; Nie et al., 1976). One could reach such generalities from one or two items glimpsed en route to the sports page just as well as from dedicated perusal of the *New York Times*. Under this scenario, the media could be very influential, but their impact would be invisible to us, since it wouldn't show up when frequent and infrequent users were

---

*Though Robinson's idea is interesting, note that his evidence is strictly circumstantial: support for women's rights happened to rise at the same time that *The Mary Tyler Moore Show* premiered. A more concrete link is needed to support his conclusion; one could just as plausibly blame the Equal Rights Amendment's ratification troubles on the appearance of *Laverne and Shirley*.

Again, while intuition tells us that prime-time television has some impact on its audience, proof is hard to come by. I examined data from the National Opinion Research Center's 1977 General Social Survey, which asked respondents how many hours of television they watched daily, and found no significant relationship between television viewing and political participation or attitudes about public policy (unpublished manuscript, 1981).

compared*. Information or ideas transmitted from frequent to infrequent users in a two-step flow might also be invisible.

A similar problem occurs when we try to compare respondents who turn first to television for news with those who depend upon newspapers or magazines. We can ascertain whether users of print media display more or less of something than broadcast users. Again, however, characteristics atttributable to media exposure get lost in the shuffle if they are exhibited equally by both groups. This difficulty plagues Robinson's "videomalaise" research: by 1972, the misanthropic attitudes once associated with viewing television news spread to users of all media, because, Robinson argues, "the effects of television journalism were so broad-based that they in turn altered the other news media" (1977: 35).

So our intuition about the media's impact on voting deserves another look. We need to learn more about the situations in which the press affects politics — and about the situations in which it doesn't.

What conditions might alter the media's influence on politics? I have suggested three major elements: the *format* in which communication takes place, the *context* in which it transpires, and the *content* of its message (Blomquist, 1981).

The format of communication involves two considerations: the technology being used and the style in which messages are presented. No doubt Marshall McLuhan was partially correct when he claimed that "the medium is the message"; each medium has peculiar strengths and weaknesses in conveying ideas. For instance, while television's visual aspect gives it a unique "you are there" quality (intensified, one presumes, with color television), newspapers and magazines probably can explain involved concepts more easily. The manner of delivery is part of the message, too. Future research will want to examine such issues as whether "hard news" is more effective than features, entertainment, or advertising, and whether brash tabloids like Rupert Murdoch's *New York Post* bestow different impressions of the world than traditional newspapers.

The context of communication is the political environment in which it occurs. The most fundamental component of this environment, of course, is the nature of the audience: who is receiving the communication and why have they chosen to do so? Another component is the structural setting — the ideology and scope of the social order in which a medium operates, and the extent to which a medium is part of that order. One suspects, for example, that the press's performance varies in authoritarian and democratic situations, in nations and municipalities, in places where editors are part of the regime and places where they are not. Finally, different types of political issues may involve different decision-making mechanisms which do not respond to the press in the same way. When policy benefits only a few, it is likely to be forged by interest groups,

*Of course, we could compare respondents who reported any amount of media use with those who reported no media use whatsoever. But there are so few individuals in the latter category that any attempt to test controls would be statistically unreliable in a sample of 1,500 respondents.

bureaucrats, and legislative staffers, with scant attention to or from the press; but when policy benefits most, the press is generally an active participant.

The content of communication — the information transmitted by the media — varies in several general aspects (obviously, the particular substance of each message is unique). First, messages differ in clarity: some communications put ideas more understandably than others. Presumably, the plainer the statement, the more likely it is to influence behavior. The social distance of the message from its audience — the extent to which the audience can identify with the problem or situation being discussed — is also a factor. Foreign policy affects everyone, but few voters care much about it except in times of crisis; therefore, press coverage of routine international affairs probably has very little impact on public opinion. The message's familiarity matters as well: the press probably is more influential when it talks about things its audience doesn't know well and when its new information is consistent with what the audience already knows. In addition, the press will likely have more effect when its message calls for only a small amount of behavioral change.

All of this adds up to a formidable research agenda which is too involved to be implemented in multipurpose surveys like the NES. Consequently, studies which concentrate on specific events — like Bradley Greenberg's survey following the assassination of John Kennedy or Sidney Kraus's work on presidential debates (1962, 1979) — should assume a more important role in mass communication research. Focused case studies can examine varieties of media influence more efficiently, less expensively, and perhaps with greater accuracy than the NES.

Nevertheless, improving survey analyses is only the beginning of the task which confronts mass communication researchers. Although we have directed our attention here to the media's impact on public opinion, we must remember that the process of electing a president involves much more than voters and voting. Ultimately, it may be in these other activities — the actions in which politicians decide to run for the White House, obtain resources from party activists, and secure party nominations — that the press has its greatest impact on election outcomes. Let us consider them briefly.

2. The press in the electoral process

In the end, the race for president is decided by who gets the most votes on Election Day. But before the polls open on the first Tuesday in leap-year Novembers, there have been many other decisions; the November voter picks from only two or three of the dozens of men and women who aspire to the presidency.

Relatively few Americans contribute to these initial selections. No more than one in a hundred attends the chicken-dinner fundraisers in backwater Holiday Inns which are the first tests of presidential mettle. The opening electoral skirmishes, the primaries, attract only a quarter of the electorate.

But at every step of the long march to the White House, from Georgetown cocktail parties to New Hampshire snows to the stairs of the Capitol on January

20, the press is there. What it does and says matters in presidential politics long before public opinion starts to form. For it is the press which maintains the "scorecard" of who's in and who's out of the running — and all signs indicate that this scorekeeping task is increasing in importance with each election.

Launching campaigns. The first phase of presidential selection begins almost as soon as balloting for the previous election finishes: would-be contenders strike out to attract sufficient support to launch national campaigns. The competition is keen. There is no dearth of politicians who would like to be president, yet the resources needed for a serious challenge — money, backing from other politicians, organizational skill — are in short supply.

During this period, the candidates' targets are the activists, the men and women for whom politics is an ongoing avocation rather than a quadrennial curiosity. In order to enter the primaries with a reasonable chance of victory, a candidate must convince enough activists that he or she can be president. More exactly, the candidate must convince activists of three things. First, the candidate must show them that his or her attitudes agree with theirs. Second, the candidate must demonstrate that he or she has the skills and temperament Americans expect of a president. Third, the candidate must persuade them that he or she can win the election.

Press coverage is a useful — perhaps imperative — means for candidates to reach activists. These early months of campaigning run on a shoestring; candidates ordinarily cannot afford to take their message directly to many whom they need to have hear it. But everywhere candidates themselves cannot appear, the press can carry impressions of policy positions, of diligent and dedicated public service, of a winner. In places where candidates cannot present their views on public policy in person, an interview with *Time* or *Newsweek* will make activists take notice. Where candidates need to establish themselves as capable leaders, a *60 Minutes* profile can authenticate their claim. Where they must back up their assertion that they can defeat the opposition, a few approving words in David Broder's *Washington Post* column may do the trick.

Items which assess a candidate's character and electability are crucial. Reporters are not necessarily wiser observers of politics than professional politicians. Yet their assessments are likely to carry more weight. Outside their own constituencies or party, most politicians are fairly obscure. But nearly everybody watches or reads the media. This is what makes the press's assessment of the political score "official." Other than the election returns themselves, the press's tote is the only one that everyone acknowledges — even if they do not always agree with it.

Getting recognized by the press can work political miracles. Twelve months before the 1976 election, Jimmy Carter was all but a nobody — a one-term southern governor, out of office for a year, without a single nationally-recognized accomplishment. Yet he had a shrewd knack for spotting opportunities. In October, 1975, the Iowa Democratic party invited all the presidential hopefuls to appear at a fundraiser. Carter guessed that the national press — having missed early indications of George McGovern's popularity four years before in Iowa — would show up en masse to catch whatever rumblings it could. When he learned that the *Des Moines Register* planned to poll Democrats attending the dinner about whom they supported, Carter set out to pack the hall (Witcover, 1978: 214). The tactic was brilliant. Carter won the largest share of the straw vote — 23 percent of the 1100 dinner guests — and was "discovered" by the media. Wrote R.W. Apple of the *New York Times:* Carter "appears to have taken a surprising but solid lead" (quoted in *Ibid.:* 215). Suddenly, the nobody was the man to beat.

"Winnowing" the field*. The second phase of presidential politics is the most grueling. Primary season opens in New Hampshire the last Tuesday in February. Every seven days for the following four months, each candidate's future goes on the line. There is no time to reflect, no chance to lick wounds, no room to make mistakes. There is only enough time to win and to lose.

Naturally, press coverage can have the same effects on voters in primary elections that it has in the fall contest. But primary voters are a different breed. The obvious difference is that voters in primaries are partisans: most states do not allow Republicans to vote in the Democratic primary or vice versa, and exclude independents entirely. Typically, however, primary voters aren't ordinary partisans. They are super-partisans — men and women who are exceptionally devoted to the ideals which separate Republicans and Democrats. Nelson Polsby and Aaron Wildavsky (1976) call them "purists," for they are more concerned with keeping their moral standards pure than with winning elections.

As we have seen, people who are so highly motivated are less likely to be affected by what they read or watch in the media. On the other hand, the campaign's issues and personalities are still fresh during primary season; there is a greater chance that voters — even "purists" — will not yet have formed attitudes about everything and everyone involved. The extent of the trade-off is unknown, because survey research into attitude change during primaries is virtually non-existent**.

Certainly it doesn't hurt to be labeled a success by the scorekeepers in the press. Again, the classic recent example is the 1976 Carter campaign. Throughout the primaries, Carter was hardly an overwhelming or consistent winner: he was soundly defeated in several major states, including New York and California, and carried others only by narrow margins. But he was the closest thing to a front-runner in the race, and thus the press seized upon him — thereby creating something of a self-fulfilling prophecy.

Carter's biggest leaps in the national polls coincided with primary triumphs that were highly touted in the press. In January, 1976, Carter stood fourth in

*I borrow this phrase from Matthews, 1978.
**Though not for long. In another section of the 1980 National Election Study, about 1,000 respondents were interviewed four times between January and November. Data from this year-long "panel," which is discussed in a companion SETUPS by Richard Joslyn and Janet Johnson (1982), should shed some light on how the media's impact differs over the course of a campaign. In addition, news organizations which conduct "exit polls" after primaries are for the first time making that data available to scholars.

the Gallup Poll, well behind George Wallace and Hubert Humphrey and slightly in back of Henry Jackson (see figure 1). A month later, after emerging from New Hampshire as the media's front-runner, Carter promptly gained 12 percentage points. Two weeks thereafter, following an appearance on the cover of *Time* and a three-point defeat of George Wallace in Florida (interpreted by the media as a stunning victory), Carter picked up another 10 percent, and stood neck-and-neck with Humphrey. Similar improvements followed two other victories which impressed the press corps, Pennsylvania on April 27 and Ohio on June 8.

Moreover, once Carter was ordained the leader, other candidates found resources increasingly difficult to come by. By April, Carter was spending as much as Jackson, Wallace, and Jerry Brown combined (Matthews, 1978: 74).

This "winner-take-all" frame of mind has enormous implications for presidential politics. It places a tremendous burden on candidates to win early, since those who do not carry Iowa, Maine, New Hampshire, or Florida find it

Figure 1. Selected Gallup Poll Democratic presidential preferences, January-June, 1976

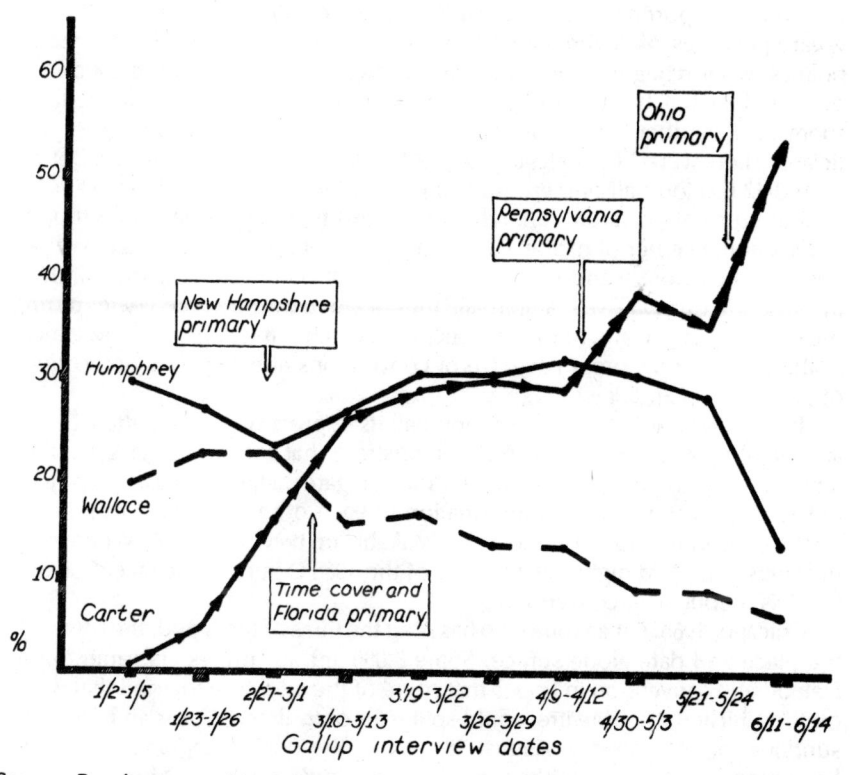

Source: Results reported in Gallup, 1978

almost impossible to catch up. In essence, it means that party nominations are determined in less than two months. Consequently, there is no room for candidates whose appeals are based on complexities; there is only enough time for rhetoric that is well-spoken and easily comprehended. And, of course, the pressures imposed by the media's mentality only add to the media's importance. With so little opportunity for traditional campaigning, candidates become more dependent than ever upon news stories and advertising to get their message across to voters.

Most reporters recognize that covering elections like horse races has harmful effects. Most of them continue to do it anyway. Journalists measure each other by their ability to manufacture order out of chaos — to take complicated situations and explain them in simple, straightforward prose. As they see it, an orderly story about an election demands a winner, some losers, and a clear result. If that formula injures the system, most would say that the system ought to be changed, rather than their style of reporting about it (see, for example, Witcover, 1978: 690-693). Such righteousness is not unusual in American journalism; indeed, the arrogant tenacity with which reporters defend their norms explains much of the ill will between politicians and the press.

Nominating conventions. Perhaps the supreme effort at bringing order out of chaos is reporting a national party convention. Conventions are the last great spectacles of American politics — the last survivors of the age when politics was torchlight parades and whistle-stop rallies. Once these spectacles belonged to the bosses, the power brokers in the legendary smoke-filled rooms. Today, they belong as much, if not more, to the media than to politicians. There were 2,000 delegates to the 1980 Republican convention in Detroit — and 12,000 journalists there watching them (Smith and Rudolph, 1980: 54).

But conventions aren't entirely hoopla and frivolity. By giving each party a week at the center of national attention, conventions help mobilize partisan ties in the electorate and raise the level of political interest. Nearly a fifth of the voters in our 1980 NES sample said they decided between candidates during the conventions. Again, however, specific research is missing: we know almost nothing about how press coverage of conventions affects public perceptions of parties and candidates.

Perceptions inside the convention hall itself are a different matter. Events at several recent party gatherings demonstrate that the media have become a means outside the party apparatus for delegates, state caucuses, and candidate organizations to pass information to each other. The media's potency on the convention floor was most unmistakable on two memorable Wednesday evenings: the third nighttime sessions of the 1968 Democratic convention and the 1980 Republican convention.

Chicago, 1968. For anyone who has seen the films of the blood, the brutality, the place and date alone suffice. Some 5,000 antiwar protesters came to the Democratic convention in hopes that some of the attention focused that week on the Chicago Ampitheatre would spill over onto them. About an hour after sundown on Wednesday, August 28, just as the nominating speeches were beginning inside the Ampitheatre, Mayor Richard J. Daley's police moved in outside. A column of several hundred officers, wielding billy clubs and Mace, invaded Grant Park, the center of protest activity. When the rush ended 30 minutes later, Grant Park was a gory mess, the air heavy with the sharp, pungent smell of tear gas (White, 1969; Royko, 1971).

The first pictures of the Grant Park confrontation appeared on the networks within the hour. As voters from coast to coast watched and gasped in horror, so did delegates and party leaders, crowded around portable sets on the convention floor. The chairman of the Colorado delegation interrupted the speeches to ask if there was any convention rule "under which Mayor Daley can be compelled to suspend the police state terror being perpetrated at this minute on kids in front of the Conrad Hilton." A delegate from Wisconsin moved to adjourn the convention and switch it to another city (Royko, 1971: 188-190). Somehow the session managed to hold together long enough to nominate Hubert Humphrey to be president, but with all pretenses of party unity irrevocably shattered.

As speaker after speaker in the Ampitheatre berated the ruthlessness of the Chicago police, Daley made no public reply (though the cameras caught him screaming "go home" to Sen. Abraham Ribicoff of Connecticut, who compared Daley's officers to the Gestapo). When he chose to answer them the following night, he did so not from the Ampitheatre rostrum, but in an interview with CBS anchorman Walter Cronkite.

Twelve years later, the Republican convention turned into a rumor mill after another Walter Cronkite interview. Toward the end of the primaries, Reagan pollster Richard Wirthlin conducted surveys which found that the most popular running mate for Reagan would be former president Gerald Ford (Germond and Witcover, 1981: ch. 8). Reagan visited Ford on the first day of the convention, discovered that the animosities left over from 1976 had disappeared, and authorized Wirthlin, campaign manager William Casey, and chief of staff Ed Meese to negotiate with Ford. The negotiations were no longer a secret by the convention's third day, Wednesday, July 16, when Ford came to CBS's anchor booth in the rafters of Detroit's Joe Louis Arena to talk with Cronkite live on the dinner-hour newscast.

A draft for the vice-presidency from the convention floor "would be tough" to reject, Ford admitted. But the decision wouldn't be that simple, he told Cronkite. "I would not go to Washington . . . and be a figurehead vice-president," he said. "I have to go there with the belief that I will play a meaningful role across the board . . . I have to have responsible assurances" (quoted in Ibid.: 182).

Ford's statement whipped the arriving delegates into a frenzy: so the "dream ticket," Reagan-Ford, was possible after all! The television reports sparked gossip on the floor, which network correspondents — under heavy pressure from their superiors to find out quickly whether the ticket was on or off — picked up and relayed as gospel. Within a couple hours, CBS, ABC, and the wire services were reporting that a deal had been made.

Word of the "dream ticket" stampede caused alarm back in Reagan's hotel suite. It was increasingly clear to the Reagan team that a settlement with Ford favorable to their candidate might not be possible. Yet, as Reagan press aide Lyn Nofziger later recalled, "you were fast reaching a time where, had it gone much longer, it would have been very difficult to not go with Ford irrespective of the conditions he might lay down. It would have looked like a double-cross" (quoted in *Ibid.*: 187).

So Reagan called Ford and asked for a decision that night. After an hour's thought, Ford declined the offer. The Reagan staff scrambled to find George Bush, the number-two choice — and to leak the news of his selection to the media before Reagan made a formal announcement at the arena. "We didn't want (delegates) to have any sort of massive expression of regret or joy either way on the governor's decision," explained Reagan convention manager William Timmons. "So we scooped him a little on the floor to settle the delegates down" (quoted in *Ibid.*: p. 189). In other words, Reagan's aides decided that use of the press was the best way to dispel what the press had wrought.

The general election campaign. Most of this SETUPS considered the potential impact of the press on voters in the fall campaign; we need not repeat those findings here. You should notice, however, that the potential for influence on party activists and campaign planning that we have observed in earlier phases of the process persists into the fall drive. Most notably, that "official score" maintained by the media continues to affect fund raising and candidates' strategy until it is finally replaced on Election Day with the one truly official score.

3. A conclusion — at a beginning

Ending this research agenda here is an arbitrary but necessary choice. We could go on for pages more, for mass communication research is rife with unexplored frontiers. And new frontiers are materializing constantly as technology leaves the laboratory and enters the marketplace.

One new frontier is of special interest. Every day, technicians connect several hundred more homes to the latest mass medium, cable television. Though the industry is still in its infancy, it already is clear that cable will evoke dramatic changes in the ways we live and work — and in how we conduct our politics.

Cable will expand the number of channels available to the average viewer from half a dozen to several score. Since it runs on a subscription basis, like newspapers and magazines, cable will be able to support programs with specialized audiences — including more in-depth broadcast news. There is already one round-the-clock news service, appropriately called Cable News Network, available on many cable systems. As of this writing, one more venture is in the works: ABC and Group W, the broadcasting division of Westinghouse, have announced plans for a cable service offering extended news reports, interview shows in the fashion of *Meet the Press*, and documentaries*.

---

*These rumblings are shaking traditional television journalism, too. ABC introduced a late-night newscast called *Nightline* in 1980, and by the time you read these words, the 60-minute evening news program — long sought by network news departments — may be reality at last.

But cable can do more than carry additional programs. The most recent installations allow viewers to "talk back" to their cable system. By pressing buttons attached to the TV set, these cable users can send messages to a central computer.

So far, this capability has been used largely for commercial functions. Some cable subscribers, for example, can pay bills over the wire; the cable company's computer contacts a computer at the subscriber's bank and debits his or her checking account.

Yet there is potential for much, much more. NBC has used the QUBE two-way cable system in Columbus, Ohio to stage "instant referenda" on political events. The preferences of each viewer in such "videopolls" can be stored in the system's computer. Someday, these records may be made available to political candidates, much as magazines like *The New Republic* and *National Review* sell their mailing lists. Indeed, just as candidates now use direct mail to reach important small groups, eventually they may use "direct television" — TV ads that would only be seen by certain selected viewers.

In the most far-reaching shift, more and more newspapers are using cable to deliver news. Newspapers will never be entirely supplanted by cable; printed messages have advantages for many advertisers (for example, try to cut out a coupon from a TV screen). On the other hand, the delays inherent in printing and distributing newspapers insure that even the freshest paper will be somewhat out of date. So many newspapers have arranged with cable systems in their area to carry updates on breaking stories, delivered to the subscriber's screen in an instant instead of hours.

It is impossible to say now just what influence these developments will ultimately have on politics. One can, nevertheless, predict several areas where controversy is likely to arise.

Cable surely will reinforce some of the changes in politics attributable to over-the-air television. After all, television news is television news: whether delivered by a wire or in the electromagnetic spectrum, the medium's predilection for events that have a strong visual component remains.

Yet in other respects, cable television will be very different than conventional broadcasting. The enhanced number of channels and talk-back capability will permit audiences to be more choosy about what they watch. It is technically feasible, for example, to design a cable system that would enable viewers to filter out news stories about subjects which don't interest them. Cable may therefore make selective exposure more selective.

Cable's talk-back power has some frightening aspects. One great shortcoming of American politics is that it often produces governments whose foresight extends no farther than the next election. How will that fault be aggravated when we can hold electronic plebiscites at the drop of a hat? How will leaders deal with the pressures of being watched and evaluated more intimately than ever? In addition, civil liberties attorneys are concerned about who will have access to the subscriber records in cable company computers. Should the government — or anyone else — be able to find out whether someone watches radical lectures, X-rated movies, or the Boston Red Sox?

Finally, there is the question of whether cable will add to "videomalaise," the misanthropy and alienation Robinson found in frequent television viewers (1976). Certainly it is conceivable that if more and more of life can be conducted from a box in the living room, one may not feel as compelled to worry about the outside world.

But now we are back where we started this agenda: raising questions faster than we can supply answers. Such may be the failing — yet also the challenge and the excitement — of mass communication research for decades to come.

Codebook

This appendix describes the subset of the 1980 American National Election Study that has been developed for use with this SETUPS*. The data file consists of 101 variables for each of the 1408 respondents in the traditional time series portion of the NES for whom both pre-election and post-election interviews were completed. It was prepared from the "early release" version of the master traditional time series file produced by the study's coordinator, the Center for Political Studies of the University of Michigan (described in CPS, 1980).

Most of the variables used here have not been changed from their "early release" format. A few, however, were condensed to simplify analysis; the recoding procedures are described in the codebook entries.

Each item has been given a mnenomic name for use with SPSS or other computer statistical packages that employ alphabetic labels. Cards to produce an SPSS system file from the dataset, including variable and value labels, are available from the Inter-University Consortium.

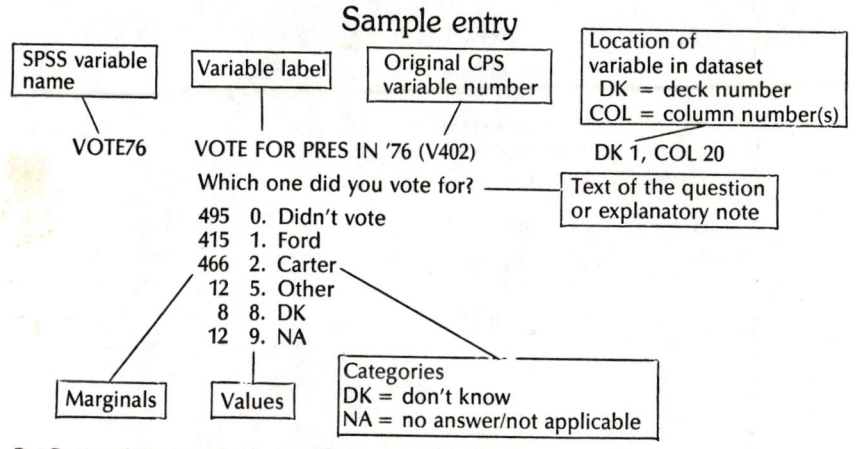

Sample entry

SPSS variable name	Variable label	Original CPS variable number	Location of variable in dataset DK = deck number COL = column number(s)

VOTE76   VOTE FOR PRES IN '76 (V402)   DK 1, COL 20
          Which one did you vote for? ── Text of the question or explanatory note
          495   0. Didn't vote
          415   1. Ford
          466   2. Carter
           12   5. Other
            8   8. DK
           12   9. NA

Categories
DK = don't know
NA = no answer/not applicable

Marginals   Values

Pat Green of the Inter-University Consortium for Political and Social Research supervised preparation of this codebook.
*SETUPS files are distributed by the Inter-University Consortium for Political and Social Research, P.O. Box 1248, Ann Arbor, Michigan 48106.

REGION	REGION OF INTERVIEW		DK 1, COL 5

This variable was originally collected and coded as the state where the interview took place. It was collapsed according to the four category census code.

    292 1. Northeast
    372 2. Midwest
    497 3. South
    247 4. West

AGE	R'S AGE IN YEARS (V465)		DK 1, COL 6-7

Month and year of R's birth subtracted from month and year of survey.
    0. NA
    18-93. Actual age of respondent

MARSTAT	R'S MARITAL STATUS (V466)		DK 1, COL 8

Are you married now and living with your (husband/wife) — or are you widowed, divorced, separated, or have you never married?

    853 1. Married
    218 2. Never married
    131 3. Divorced
      36 4. Separated
    154 5. Widowed
      16 7. Living together

RACE	R'S RACE (V706,V707)		DK 1, COL 9

Race of respondent.

    1181 1. White
     162 2. Black
      48 3. Hispanic
      17 4. Other

INCOME	TOTAL INCOME OF R'S HOUSEHOLD (V637,V638)		DK 1, COL 10

Combined income of all family members in 1979.

    327 1. $0 — $9,999
    468 2. $10,000 — $22,999
    467 3. $23,000 and over
    146 9. DK or NA

EDUC	R'S EDUCATION (V486)		DK 1, COL 11

Highest level of education attained by R.

    344 1. Less than high school degree
    515 2. High school degree
    545 3. Some college
       4 9. DK or NA

RELIG	R'S RELIGIOUS PREFERENCE (V644)		DK 1, COL 12

Is your religious preference Protestant, Roman Catholic, Jewish or something else?

    605 1. Protestant
    240 2. Fundamentalist

	50	3. Minor Christian	
	318	4. Catholic	
	41	5. Jewish	
	23	6. Other	
	119	7. No preference	
	12	9. NA	

CLASS   R'S PERCEIVED SOCIAL CLASS (V642)   DK 1, COL 13

Summary: R's subjective social class.

       673   1. Working class
       641   2. Middle and upper class
       94   9. DK or NA

SEX   R'S SEX (V705)   DK 1, COL 14

Respondent's sex.

       615   1. Male
       793   2. Female

OCC   R'S OCCUPATION (V504)   DK 1, COL 15

What is your main occupation? (What sort of work do you do?)

       533   0. NA or not currently working
       160   1. Professional or technical
       179   2. Sales
       140   3. Clerical
       113   4. Crafts
       89   5. Operatives
       25   6. Transportation
       29   7. Laborers
       17   8. Farm
       123   9. Service

WORKING   R'S WORK STATUS (V567)   DK 1, COL 16

Summary: R's working status

       849   1. Works 20 or more hours per week
       11   2. Temporarily laid off
       65   4. Unemployed
       185   5. Retired
       41   6. Permanently disabled
       215   7. Housewife
       42   8. Student

RELIGIMP   IS RELIGION IMPORTANT TO R? (V1172)   DK 1, COL 17

Do you consider religion to be an important part of your life or not?

       1052   1. Yes
       346   5. No
       6   8. DK
       4   9. NA

PARTYID   R'S PARTY IDENTIFICATION (V278)   DK 1, COL 18

Summary: R's Party I.D.

       245   0. Strong Democrat

```
317   1. Weak Democrat
161   2. Independent — leans toward Democrat
176   3. Independent
150   4. Independent — leans toward Republican
202   5. Weak Republican
127   6. Strong Republican
  1   7. Other - Minor party
 28   8. Apolitical
  1   9. DK or NA
```

VOTED76 DID R VOTE FOR PRES IN '76 (V401) DK 1, COL 19

Now, in 1976 you remember that Gerald Ford ran on the Republican ticket against Jimmy Carter for the Democrats. Do you remember for sure whether or not you voted in that election?

```
306   0. Never votes
913   1. Yes
154   5. No
 31   7. Don't recall
  4   9. NA
```

VOTE76 VOTE FOR PRES IN '76 (V402) DK 1, COL 20

Which one did you vote for?

```
495   0. Didn't vote
415   1. Ford
466   2. Carter
 12   5. Other
  8   8. DK
 12   9. NA
```

PARTISAN STRENGTH OF R'S PARTISANSHIP (V278) DK 1, COL 21

This variable was recoded from PARTYID.

```
372   1. Strong party identification
519   2. Weak party identification
311   3. Independent - leaning
176   4. Independent
 30   9. DK or NA
```

INFO R'S CAMPAIGN INFORMATION LEVEL DK 1, COL 22

This index was derived from questions requiring knowledge of candidates' issue stands and election outcomes. First, respondents were asked for the positions of Jimmy Carter and Ronald Reagan on six issues — increasing defense spending, reducing overall government spending, abortion, cutting taxes, getting along with the Soviet Union, and women's rights. Respondents received one point for each time they perceived Carter's issue stance as more liberal than Reagan's — that is, if they thought Carter's position was closer to reducing defense spending, maintaining government services, choice on abortion, keeping taxes at current levels, pursuing detente, and supporting an equal role for women. Respondents also received one point if they knew whether the incumbent was running for the House of Representatives from their district and could identify him or her, if they knew Democrats controlled the House before the election, and/or if they knew Democrats still had a House majority after the election. The resulting zero-to-nine scale was recoded to three groups, roughly thirds.

584	1. Poorly informed
401	2. Moderately informed
423	3. Well informed

LIBCON   LIBERALISM SCALE: R'S SELF-PLACEMENT (V279)   DK 1, COL 23

We hear a lot of talk these days about liberals and conservatives. Here is a seven-point scale on which the political views that people might hold are arranged from extremely liberal to extremely conservative. Where would you place yourself on this scale or haven't you thought much about it?

420	0. Haven't thought much
22	1. Extremely liberal
84	2. Liberal
121	3. Slightly liberal
266	4. Middle of the road
188	5. Slightly conservative
181	6. Conservative
28	7. Extremely conservative
52	8. DK
46	9. NA

LIBCONJC   LIBERALISM SCALE: CARTER (V280)   DK 1, COL 24

Where would you place Jimmy Carter <liberal-conservative>?

518	0. Haven't thought much
50	1. Extremely liberal
140	2. Liberal
178	3. Slightly liberal
217	4. Middle of the road
118	5. Slightly conservative
90	6. Conservative
28	7. Extremely conservative
65	8. DK
4	9. NA

LIBCONRR   LIBERALISM SCALE: REAGAN (V281)   DK 1, COL 25

Where would you place Ronald Reagan <liberal-conservative>?

518	0. Haven't thought much
8	1. Extremely liberal
54	2. Liberal
63	3. Slightly liberal
73	4. Middle of the road
148	5. Slightly conservative
343	6. Conservative
132	7. Extremely conservative
65	8. DK
4	9. NA

LIBCONEK   LIBERALISM SCALE: KENNEDY (V282)   DK 1, COL 26

Where would you place Ted Kennedy <liberal-conservative>?

519	0. Haven't thought much
242	1. Extremely liberal
245	2. Liberal
134	3. Slightly liberal

81	4. Middle of the road
55	5. Slightly conservative
30	6. Conservative
12	7. Extremely conservative
86	8. DK
4	9. NA

LIBCONJA LIBERALISM SCALE: ANDERSON (V286)   DK 1, COL 27
Where would you place John Anderson <liberal-conservative>?

518	0. Haven't thought much
44	1. Extremely liberal
128	2. Liberal
148	3. Slightly liberal
196	4. Middle of the road
96	5. Slightly conservative
54	6. Conservative
12	7. Extremely conservative
208	8. DK
4	9. NA

LIBINDEX R'S LIBERALISM ON ISSUES   DK 1, COL 28

This index was derived from items measuring respondent's opinions on seven issues: defense spending (variable DEFENSE), size of the federal budget (CUTSPEND), inflation and unemployment (INFLUNEM), government aid to minority groups (MINOR), detente (USSR), women's rights (WOMEN) and the government's responsibility for full employment (CGETJOB). Each of these items records the respondent's opinion on a seven-point scale. Sometimes the low end of the scale represents a liberal response; sometimes a low value represents a conservative answer. In constructing this index, values from one to three were counted as liberal for variables DEFENSE, MINOR, USSR WOMEN, and CGETJOB, and as conservative for CUTSPEND and INFLUNEM. Responses from five to seven were coded the opposite, while the value four was ignored. The index was formed by subtracting the number of conservative answers from the number of liberal answers. It appears here recoded approximately into thirds.

488	1. Conservative
406	2. Middle of the road
514	3. Liberal

NOSAY PEOPLE LIKE R HAVE NO SAY (V1029)   DK 1, COL 29
People like me don't have any say about what the government does.

550	1. Agree
831	5. Disagree
22	8. DK
5	9. NA

VOTEONLY VOTING ONLY WAY FOR SAY (V1030)   DK 1, COL 30
Voting is the only way people like me can have any say about how the government runs things.

817	1. Agree
541	5. Disagree
46	8. DK
4	9. NA

COMPLEX   POLITICS TOO COMPLEX (V1031)   DK 1, COL 31
   Sometimes politics and government seem so complicated that a person like me can't really understand what's going on.
      983   1. Agree
      393   5. Disagree
       28   8. DK
        4   9. NA

DONTCARE   OFFICIALS DON'T CARE ABOUT R (V1032)   DK 1, COL 32
   I don't think public officials care much what people like me think.
      728   1. Agree
      607   5. Disagree
       62   8. DK
       11   9. NA

LOSETUCH   CONGRESSMEN LOSE TOUCH WITH VOTERS (V1033)   DK 1, COL 33
   Generally speaking, those we elect to Congress in Washington lose touch with the people pretty quickly.
      990   1. Agree
      323   5. Disagree
       81   8. DK
       14   9. NA

WANTVOTE   PARTIES ONLY WANT VOTES (V1034)   DK 1, COL 34
   Parties are only interested in people's votes but not in their opinions.
      823   1. Agree
      495   5. Disagree
       82   8. DK
        8   9. NA

EFFSCALE   POLITICAL EFFICACY INDEX   DK 1, COL 35
   This variable was derived by counting the number of times the respondent agreed with the statements in variables NOSAY, VOTEONLY, COMPLEX, DONTCARE, LOSETUCH, and WANTVOTE, and recoding the results approximately into thirds.
      447   1. High efficacy
      494   2. Medium efficacy
      467   3. Low efficacy

WHOLLWIN   R'S OPINION: PROBABLE WINNER (V12)   DK 1, COL 36
   Who do you think will be elected President in November?
      545   1. Reagan
      643   2. Carter
        5   3. Anderson
      167   8. DK
       48   9. NA

CAREWHO   R CARE ABOUT OUTCOME? (V19)   DK 1, COL 37
   Generally speaking, would you say that you personally care a good deal

which party wins the presidential election this fall, or that you don't care very much which party wins?

  762 1. Care a good deal
  557 3. Don't care very much
   35 8. DK
   54 9. NA

PROBVOTE R'S PRE-ELEC PRES PREFERENCE (V140) DK 1, COL 38

Who do you think you will vote for in the election for President?

  537 1. Carter
  504 5. Reagan
  113 6. Anderson
   23 7. Other
  163 8. DK
   68 9. NA or won't vote

VOTED80 DID R VOTE IN '80 (V992) DK 1, COL 39

Did you vote for a candidate for President?

  404 0. NA
  996 1. Yes
    8 5. No

VOTE80 VOTE FOR PRES IN '80 (V993) DK 1, COL 40

Who did you vote for?

  412 0. Did not vote
  494 1. Reagan
  383 2. Carter
   10 5. Clark
   81 6. Anderson
    4 7. Other
   16 8. DK
    8 9. NA

WHENPICK WHEN DID R DECIDE HOW TO VOTE? (V995) DK 1, COL 41-42

How long before the election did you decide that you were going to vote the way you did?

  412 0. Did not vote
  199 1. Knew all along
  110 2. Before the conventions
  120 3. During the GOP convention
   59 4. During the Democratic convention
   77 5. After the conventions
   15 6. Five to seven weeks before the election
   58 7. One month before the election
   94 8. Two weeks before the election
   69 9. Last days before the election
   92 10. Election day
   91 11. During the primaries
     Other = 97 (4); DK = 98 (3); NA = 99 (5)

CHGMIND DID R CHANGE CHOICE OVER CAMPAIGN? DK 1, COL 43

This variable was derived by comparing PROBVOTE and VOTE80.

103   0. Yes
721   1. No
584   9. NA

NONELEC   NUMBER OF NON-ELECTORAL ACTIVITIES   DK 1, COL 44

This variable was derived by counting the number of these activities performed by the respondent: trying to persuade someone else to vote for a particular party or candidate (CPS V792), attending any political function (V794), working for a party or candidate (V795), wearing a campaign button or placing a bumper sticker on their car (V796), and belonging to a political club or other political organization.

832   0. None
425   1. One
99   2. Two
34   3. Three
11   4. Four
7   5. Five

INTEREST   INTEREST IN CAMPAIGN (V743)   DK 1, COL 45

Some people don't pay much attention to campaigns. How about you? Would you say that you were very much interested, somewhat interested, or not much interested in following the political campaigns this year?

 04   1. Very much interested
32   . Somewhat interested
 70   5. Not much interested
2   9. NA

PRESPOP   ASSESSMENT OF CARTER'S PERFORMANCE (V23)   DK 1, COL 46

Do you approve or disapprove of the way Jimmy Carter is handling his job as President?

166   1. Strongly approve
348   2. Approve
281   4. Disapprove
479   5. Strongly disapprove
4   8. DK
130   9. NA

PREJC   PRE-ELEC THERM: CARTER (V157)   DK 1, COL 47-49

I'll read the name of a person and I'd like you to rate that person using this feeling thermometer. You may use any number from 0 to 100 for rating. Ratings between 50 and 100 mean that you feel favorable towards the person. Ratings between 0 and 50 degrees mean that you don't feel favorable toward the person. If we come to a name that you don't recognize, you don't need to rate that person. If you do recognize the name but don't feel particularly warm or cold toward the person, you would rate the person at the 50 degree mark. How would you rate Jimmy Carter using the feeling thermometer?

0-49. Unfavorable
50. Not particularly warm or cold
51-100. Favorable
997. R doesn't recognize name
998. DK where to rate; can't judge
999. NA

PRERR   PRE-ELEC THERM: REAGAN (V158)   DK 1, COL 50-52

             0-49. Unfavorable
              50. Not particularly warm or cold
             51-100. Favorable
             997. R doesn't recognize name
             998. DK where to rate; can't judge
             999. NA

PREEK   PRE-ELEC THERM: KENNEDY (V159)   DK 1, COL 53-55

             0-49. Unfavorable
              50. Not particularly warm or cold
             51-100. Favorable
             997. R doesn't recognize name
             998. DK where to rate; can't judge
             999. NA

PREJA   PRE-ELEC THERM: ANDERSON (V166)   DK 1, COL 56-58

             0-49. Unfavorable
              50. Not particularly warm or cold
             51-100. Favorable
             997. R doesn't recognize name
             998. DK where to rate; can't judge
             999. NA

POSTJC   POST-ELEC THERM: CARTER (V843)   DK 1, COL 59-61

             0-49. Unfavorable
              50. Not particularly warm or cold
             51-100. Favorable
             997. R doesn't recognize name
             998. DK where to rate; can't judge
             999. NA

POSTRR   POST-ELEC THERM: REAGAN (V844)   DK 1, COL 62-64

             0-49. Unfavorable
              50. Not particularly warm or cold
             51-100. Favorable
             997. R doesn't recognize name
             998. DK where to rate; can't judge
             999. NA

POSTEK   POST-ELEC THERM: KENNEDY (V845)   DK 1, COL 65-67

             0-49. Unfavorable
              50. Not particularly warm or cold
             51-100. Favorable
             997. R doesn't recognize name
             998. DK where to rate; can't judge
             999. NA

POSTJA   POST-ELEC THERM: ANDERSON (V846)   DK 1, COL 68-70

             0-49. Unfavorable

50. Not particularly warm or cold
51-100. Favorable
997. R doesn't recognize name
998. DK where to rate; can't judge
999. NA

MORALRR   DESCRIBE REAGAN AS MORAL? (V422)   DK 1, COL 71
How does the word moral describe Reagan?
- 222   1. Extremely well
- 683   2. Quite well
- 289   3. Not too well
- 60   4. Not well at all
- 94   8. DK
- 60   9. NA

KNOWRR   DESCRIBE REAGAN AS KNOWLEDGEABLE? (V425)   DK 1, COL 72
How does knowledgeable describe Reagan?
- 279   1. Extremely well
- 633   2. Quite well
- 282   3. Not too well
- 103   4. Not well at all
- 52   8. DK
- 59   9. NA

POWERRR   DESCRIBE REAGAN AS POWER-HUNGRY? (V426)   DK 1, COL 73
How does power-hungry describe Reagan?
- 329   1. Extremely well
- 378   2. Quite well
- 331   3. Not too well
- 222   4. Not well at all
- 87   8. DK
- 61   9. NA

SOLVECRR   DESCRIBE REAGAN AS ECON PROBLEM-SOLVER?(V428) DK 1, COL 74
How does he would solve our economic problems describe Reagan?
- 51   1. Extremely well
- 456   2. Quite well
- 515   3. Not too well
- 198   4. Not well at all
- 129   8. DK
- 59   9. NA

LEADERRR   DESCRIBE REAGAN AS A LEADER? (V429)   DK 1, COL 75
How does he would provide strong leadership describe Reagan?
- 196   1. Extremely well
- 565   2. Quite well
- 331   3. Not too well
- 162   4. Not well at all
- 96   8. DK
- 58   9. NA

FORNRR   DESCRIBE REAGAN AS GOOD FOR FORN REL? (V430)   DK 1, COL 76

How does he would develop good relations with other countries describe Reagan?

  85 1. Extremely well
 466 2. Quite well
 417 3. Not too well
 225 4. Not well at all
 156 8. DK
  59 9. NA

MORALJA DESCRIBE ANDERSON AS MORAL? (V431) DK 1, COL 77

How does moral describe John Anderson?

 182 1. Extremely well
 518 2. Quite well
 142 3. Not too well
  57 4. Not well at all
 407 8. DK
 102 9. NA

KNOWJA DESCRIBE ANDERSON AS KNO/L U/ G.BLE ' / /434) X O' /3

How does knowledgeable describe Anderson?

 145 1. Extremely well
 562 2. Quite well
 241 3. Not too well
  27 4. Not well at all
 329 8. DK
 104 9. NA

POWERJA DESCRIBE ANDERSON AS POWER-HUNGRY (V435) DK 1, COL 79

How does power-hungry describe Anderson?

 115 1. Extremely well
 272 2. Quite well
 399 3. Not too well
 152 4. Not well at all
 365 8. DK
 105 9. NA

SOLVECJA DESCRIBE ANDERSON AS ECON PROBLEM- DK 2, COL 5
     SOLVER? (V437)

How does he would solve our economic problems describe Anderson?

  19 1. Extremely well
 201 2. Quite well
 486 3. Not too well
 182 4. Not well at all
 416 8. DK
 104 9. NA

LEADERJA DESCRIBE ANDERSON AS A LEADER? (V438) DK 2, COL 6

How does he would provide strong leadership describe Anderson?

  43 1. Extremely well
 341 2. Quite well
 378 3. Not too well

159	4. Not well at all
384	8. DK
103	9. NA

FORNJA   DESCRIBE ANDERSON AS GOOD FOR FORN REL(V439) DK 2, COL 7

How does he would develop good relations with other countries describe Anderson?

37	1. Extremely well
356	2. Quite well
345	3. Not too well
116	4. Not well at all
451	8. DK
103	9. NA

MORALJC   DESCRIBE CARTER AS MORAL? (V440)   DK 2, COL 8

How does moral describe Carter?

458	1. Extremely well
603	2. Quite well
187	3. Not too well
59	4. Not well at all
43	8. DK
58	9. NA

KNOWJC   DESCRIBE CARTER AS KNOWLEDGEABLE? (V443)   DK 2, COL 9

How does knowledgeable describe Carter?

293	1. Extremely well
691	2. Quite well
276	3. Not too well
54	4. Not well at all
35	8. DK
59	9. NA

POWERJC   DESCRIBE CARTER AS POWER-HUNGRY? (V444)   DK 2, COL 10

How does power-hungry describe Carter?

191	1. Extremely well
345	2. Quite well
469	3. Not too well
287	4. Not well at all
58	8. DK
58	9. NA

SOLVECJC   DESCRIBE CARTER AS ECON PROBLEM-SOLVER? (V446) DK 2, COL 11

How does he would solve our economic porblems describe Carter?

43	1. Extremely well
248	2. Quite well
590	3. Not too well
419	4. Not well at all
51	8. DK
57	9. NA

LEADERJC   DESCRIBE CARTER AS A LEADER? (V447)   DK 2, COL 12

How does he would provide strong leadership describe Carter?

   74 1. Extremely well
395 2. Quite well
537 3. Not too well
308 4. Not well at all
  37 8. DK
  57 9. NA

FORNJC   DESCRIBE CARTER AS GOOD FOR FORN REL? (V448)   DK 2, COL 13

How does he would develop good relations with other countries describe Carter?

175 1. Extremely well
525 2. Quite well
385 3. Not too well
217 4. Not well at all
  49 8. DK
  57 9. NA

PROBLEM   R'S OPINION: MOST IMPORTANT NATL PROB   DK 2, COL 14

What do you personally feel are the most important problems the government in Washington should try to take care of? Of those you have mentioned, which would you say is the most important problem the government in Washington should try to take care of?
This variable was collapsed from CPS V978 as follows:
10-12, 19, 60-62, 100, 109, 150-169, 211, 400-411 = 1. 5, 20-21, 30-31,39, 40-41, 50-51, 59, 90-92, 304, 833, 835-837,840, 842, 890 = 2. 46, 340-380, 810-811, 832, 871, 879, 886 = 3. 120-121, 500-599, 700-799 = 4. All other responses = 9.

807 1. Economy
  70 2. Social services
  31 3. Public order or moral concerns
436 4. Foreign affairs
  64 9. NA

TALK2OTH   TALK TO OTHERS ABOUT MOST IMP PROB? (V979)   DK 2, COL 15

During the last week or two, have you talked to other people about this problem?

785 1. Yes
557 5. No
   8 8. DK
  58 9. NA

CONCERN   CONCERN FOR MOST IMP PROB (V981)   DK 2, COL 16

Just how strongly would you say you feel about this problem?

682 1. Extremely concerned
524 2. Very concerned
134 3. Somewhat concerned
  10 4. A little concerned
   2 8. DK
  56 9. NA

READMIP   CONSULT MEDIA ON MOST IMP PROB? (V980)   DK 2, COL 17

In the last week or two, have you seen or read anything in the news about this problem?

- 1076   1. Yes
- 268   5. No
- 9   8. DK
- 55   9. NA

DEFENSE   R'S OPINION: DEFENSE SPENDING (V301)   DK 2, COL 18

Some people believe that we should spend much less money for defense. Others feel that defense spending should be greatly increased. Where would you place yourself on this scale or haven't you thought much about it?

- 165   0. Haven't thought much about it
- 35   1. Greatly decrease defense spending
- 33   2.
- 68   3.
- 211   4.
- 288   5.
- 287   6.
- 285   7. Greatly increase defense spending
- 29   8. DK
- 7   9. NA

CUTSPEND   R'S OPINION: CUT GOVERNMENT SPENDING (V321)   DK 2, COL 19

Some people think the government should provide fewer services, even in areas such as health and education, in order to reduce spending. Other people feel it is important for the government to continue the services it now provides even if it means no reduction in spending. Where would you place yourself on this scale or haven't you thought much about it?

- 173   0. Haven't thought much about it
- 95   1. Government should provide many fewer services; Reduce spending a lot.
- 129   2.
- 170   3.
- 228   4.
- 159   5.
- 166   6.
- 213   7. Government should continue to provide services; No reduction in spending.
- 67   8. DK
- 8   9. NA

INFLUNEM   R'S OPINION: INFLATION VS UNEMPLOYMENT (V341) DK 2, COL 20

Some people feel the federal government should take action to reduce the inflation rate, even if it means that unemployment would go up a lot. Others feel the government should take action to reduce the rate of unemployment, even if it means that inflation would go up a lot. Where would you place yourself on this scale or haven't you thought much about it?

- 347   0. Haven't thought much about it
- 42   1. Reduce inflation even if unemployment goes up a lot
- 67   2.
- 131   3.
- 297   4.

157	5.
69	6.
69	7. Reduce unemployment even if inflation goes up a lot
193	8. DK
36	9. NA

ABORTION   R'S OPINION: ABORTION (V351)   DK 2, COL 21

There has been some discussion about abortion during recent years. Which one of the opinions on this page best agrees with your view? You can just tell me the number of the opinion you choose.

160	1. By law, abortion should never be permitted.
436	2. The law should permit abortion only in case of rape, incest or when the woman's life is in danger.
252	3. The law should permit abortion for reasons other than rape, incest, or danger to the woman's life, but only after the need for the abortion has been clearly established.
504	4. By law, a woman should always be able to obtain an abortion as a matter of personal choice.
18	7. Other
32	8. DK
6	9. NA

TAXES   R'S OPINION: TAX RATES (V361)   DK 2, COL 22

Do you feel you are asked to pay much more than you should in federal income taxes, somewhat more than you should, about the right amount, or less than you should?

486	1. Much more
438	2. Somewhat more
327	3. About right
19	4. Less than should
125	7. Pay no taxes
6	8. DK
7	9. NA

MINOR   R'S OPINION: GOVT HELP MINORITIES? (V1061) DK 2, COL 23

Some people feel that the government in Washington should make every effort to improve the social and economic position of blacks and minority groups even if it means giving them preferential treatment. Others feel that the government should not make any special effort to help minorities because they should help themselves. Where would you place yourself on this scale or haven't you thought much about it?

168	0. Haven't thought much about it
64	1. Government should help minority groups
60	2.
138	3.
355	4.
257	5.
156	6.
173	7. Minority groups should help themselves
30	8. DK
7	9. NA

USSR   R'S OPINION: GET ALONG WITH USSR (V1077)   DK 2, COL 24

Some people feel it is important for us to try very hard to get along with Russia. Others feel it is a big mistake to try too hard to get along with Russia. Where would you place yourself on this scale or haven't you thought much about it?

173	0. Haven't thought much about it
155	1. Important to try very hard to get along with Russia
143	2.
170	3.
288	4.
165	5.
139	6.
126	7. Big mistake to try too hard to get along with Russia
44	8. DK
5	9. NA

WOMEN   R'S OPINION: ROLE FOR WOMEN (V1093)   DK 2, COL 25

Recently there has been a lot of talk about women's rights. Some people feel that women should have an equal role with men in running business, industry and government. Others feel that women's place is in the home. Where would you place yourself on this scale or haven't you thought much about it?

59	0. Haven't thought much about it
458	1. Equal role
217	2.
137	3.
224	4.
98	5.
85	6.
89	7. Women's place in home
31	8. DK
10	9. NA

CGETJOB   R'S OPINION: GOVT GUARANTEE LIVING (V1109)   DK 2, COL 26

Some people feel the government in Washington should see to it that every person has a job and a good standard of living. Others think the government should just let each person get ahead on his own. Where would you place yourself on this scale or haven't you thought much about it?

176	0. Haven't thought much about it
136	1. Government see to job and standard of living
95	2.
129	3.
246	4.
188	5.
222	6.
163	7. Government let each person get ahead on own
45	8. DK
8	9. NA

BUSING   R'S OPINION: SCHOOL BUSING (V1132)   DK 2, COL 27

There is much discussion about the best way to deal with racial problems. Some people think that achieving racial integration of schools is so important that it justifies busing children to schools out of their own neighborhoods. Others think letting children go to their own neighborhood schools is so important that they oppose busing. Where would you place yourself on this scale or haven't you thought much about it?

81	0. Haven't thought much about it
49	1. Bus to achieve integration
37	2.
39	3.
80	4.
73	5.
230	6.
795	7. Keep children in neighborhood schools
19	8. DK
5	9. NA

FEDGOVT R'S EVALUATION: FED GOVT (V761) DK 2, COL 28

Now we'd like to ask how good a job you feel some of the parts of our government are doing. As I read please give me the number that best describes how good a job you feel that part of the government is doing for the country as a whole. The Federal Government in Washington.

63	0. Very poor job
29	1.
260	2. Poor job
162	3.
603	4. Fair job
103	5.
101	6. Good job
13	7.
7	8. Very good job
67	9. No opinion

PRES R'S EVALUATION: PRESIDENCY (V764) DK 2, COL 29

The Presidency <R's rating of job performance>.

69	0. Very poor job
37	1.
255	2. Poor job
159	3.
448	4. Fair job
149	5.
176	6. Good job
22	7.
33	8. Very good job
60	9. No opinion

CONGRESS R'S EVALUATION: CONGRESS (V765) DK 2, COL 30

The Congress <R's rating of job performance>.

57	0. Very poor job
31	1.
275	2. Poor job
179	3.
444	4. Fair job
139	5.
110	6. Good job
16	7.

```
           18   8. Very good job
          139   9. No opinion
```

SCOTUS   R'S EVALUATION: SUPREME COURT (V766)   DK 2, COL 31
The Supreme Court <R's rating of job performance>.
```
           45   0. Very poor job
           46   1.
          135   2. Poor job
          122   3.
          319   4. Fair job
          143   5.
          220   6. Good job
           36   7.
           37   8. Very good job
          305   9. No opinion
```

WATCHTV   HOW OFTEN WATCH TV NEWS? (V221)   DK 2, COL 32
How often do you watch the national network news on TV?
```
          524   1. Every evening
          321   2. 3 or 4 times a week
          244   3. Once or twice a week
          199   4. Less often
           75   5. Never
           45   9. NA
```

ATTNTV   PAY ATTN TO TV POLITICAL NEWS? (V222)   DK 2, COL 33
When you watch the news on TV, do you pay a great deal of attention to news about government and politics, do you pay some attention, or don't you pay much attention to news about government and politics?
```
          104   1. Don't pay much attention
          588   3. Pay some attention
          594   5. Pay a great deal of attention
          122   9. NA
```

USERADIO   DID R USE RADIO FOR INFO? (V744)   DK 2, COL 34
Did you listen to any speeches of discussions about the campaign on the radio?
```
          659   1. Yes
          747   5. No
            2   9. NA
```

INTRADIO   INTENSITY OF RADIO USE (V745)   DK 2, COL 35
Would you say you listened to a good many <campaign radio programs>, several, or just one or two?
```
          134   1. A good many
          299   2. Several
          225   3. Just one or two
            1   8. DK
          749   9. NA; Inap., didn't listen to any
```

| USEMAGS | DID R USE MAGAZINES FOR INFO? (V746) | DK 2, COL 36 |

How about magazines — did you read about the campaign in any magazines?

```
486  1. Yes
917  5. No
  3  8. DK
  2  9. NA
```

| INTMAGS | INTENSITY OF MAGAZINE USE (V747) | DK 2, COL 37 |

How many magazine articles about the campaign would you say you read —

```
 92  1. A good many
222  2. Several
172  3. One or two
922  9. NA; Inap., R didn't read any
```

| USETV | DID R USE TV FOR INFO? (V748) | DK 2, COL 38 |

Did you watch any programs about the campaign on television?

```
1208  1. Yes
 198  5. No
   1  8. DK
   1  9. NA
```

| INTTV | INTENSITY OF TV USE (V749) | DK 2, COL 39 |

Would you say you watched —

```
329  1. A good many
532  2. Several
343  3. One or two
  1  8. DK
203  9. NA
```

| USENEWS | DID R USE NEWSPAPERS FOR INFO? (V759) | DK 2, COL 40 |

Did you read about the campaign in any newspapers?

```
993  1. Yes
407  5. No
  5  8. DK
  3  9. NA
```

| INTNEWS | INTENSITY OF NEWSPAPER USE (V760) | DK 2, COL 41 |

How many newspaper articles did you read about the campaign —

```
357  1. A good many
417  2. Several
214  3. One or two
  3  5. None
  1  8. DK
416  9. NA; Inap., didn't read any
```

| DEBATE | DID R SEE CARTER-REAGAN DEBATE? (V750) | DK 2, COL 42 |

Did you watch the televised debate between Carter and Reagan?

	974	1. Yes
	13	3. R volunteers: listened to on radio
	414	5. No
	3	8. DK
	4	9. NA

WHOWON R'S OPINION: DEBATE WINNER (V752)　　　DK 2, COL 43

Now thinking just about the debate and not the rest of the campaign, which of the two candidates impressed you as being more qualified to be President?

	421	0. Inap., didn't see the debate
	464	1. Reagan
	283	2. Carter
	134	3. Neither
	69	4. Equal
	32	8. DK
	5	9. NA

EDIT　　ENDORSEMENT OF R'S FAVORITE PAPER　　　DK 2, COL 44

This item is a recode of the respondent's newpaper usage, CPS variables V754 and V758, using endorsement data presented in *Editor and Publisher*'s newspaper poll (11/1/80: 10) supplemented by telephone interviews with editorial writers at the largest newspapers not included in the published listing. Because no attempt was made to include every newspaper named by respondents, the respondents for whom endorsements have been coded are not a random sample of voters. They should be evaluated merely as a group of newspaper readers. Most of the data for this variable was collected by Jon Kenton of Harvard College.

	147	1. Carter
	362	2. Reagan
	23	3. Anderson
	59	8. Other - No endorsement
	817	9. NA

MOSTIMP　MOST IMPORTANT SOURCE OF CAMPAIGN INFO　　DK 2, COL 45

This variable was derived from CPS variables V217-V220 and represents the medium a respondent used most for information.

	754	1. Television
	228	2. Newspapers
	44	3. Magazines
	115	4. Radio
	135	5. Combination
	73	6. All equal
	13	7. None
	2	8. DK
	44	9. NA

MEDIAUSE NUMBER MEDIA USED FOR CAMPAIGN INFO　　DK 2, COL 46

This variable was derived by counting affirmative answers to USERADIO, USEMAGS, USETV, and USENEWS.

| | 81 | 0. None |
| | 224 | 1. One |

421	2. Two
448	3. Three
234	4. Four

INTENSE   OVERALL INTENSITY OF MEDIA USE   DK 2, COL 47-48

This index was formed by adding answers to INTRADIO, INTMAGS, INTTV, and INTNEWS. Respondents received three points for each medium in which they perused "a good many" items, two points for each in which they perused "several," one point for each in which they perused "just one or two," and no points if they did not use a medium at all. The resulting scale ran from 0 to 12. It is recoded here into fourths: 0-2=10, 3-4=20, 5-6=30, 7-12=40.

371	10. Very low
330	20. Low
321	30. High
386	40. Very high

TVNEWS   R'S EVALUATION: NATIONAL TV NEWS (V768)   DK 2, COL 49

Now we'd like to ask how good a job you feel some of the parts of our government are doing. As I read please give me the number that best describes how good a job you feel that part of the government is doing for the country as a whole. The National TV News.

28	0. Very poor job
12	1.
66	2. Poor job
73	3.
292	4. Fair job
155	5.
477	6. Good job
83	7.
133	8. Very good job
89	9. No opinion

References

Agnew, Spiro. 1970. *Frankly Speaking*. Washington: Public Affairs Press.

Berelson, Bernard R., Paul F. Lazarsfeld, and William N. McPhee. 1954. *Voting*. Chicago: University of Chicago Press.

Blomquist, David. 1979. *Press and the Agency Manager*. Cambridge: Kennedy School of Government, Harvard University.

Blomquist, David. 1981. "The mass media and politics: a systems approach." Paper presented at the 1981 annual meeting, Northeastern Political Science Association.

Campbell, Angus, Gerald Gurin, and Warren E. Miller. 1953. "Television and the election." *Scientific American*, May, 1953, p. 46ff.

Center for Political Studies, Institute for Social Research, The University of Michigan. 1981. *American National Election Study, 1980: Traditional Time Series Codebook*. Ann Arbor: Center for Political Studies.

Cohen, Bernard C. 1963. *The Press and Foreign Policy*. Princeton: Princeton University Press.

Converse, Philip E. 1962. "Information flow and the stability of partisan attitudes." *Public Opinion Quarterly* 26: 578ff.

Davis, James A. 1971. *Elementary Survey Analysis*. Englewood Cliffs: Prentice-Hall.

Editor and Publisher. 1980. *Editor and Publisher Yearbook, 1980*. New York: Editor and Publisher.

Emery, Edwin. 1972. *The Press and America*. Englewood Cliffs: Prentice-Hall.

Erikson, Robert S., and Norman R. Luttbeg. 1973. *American Public Opinion*. New York: Wiley.

Epstein, Edward Jay. 1973. *News From Nowhere*. New York: Vintage.

Funkhouser, G. Ray. 1973. "The issues of the '60s." *Public Opinion Quarterly* 37: 62ff.

Gallup, George H. 1978. *The Gallup Poll: Public Opinion, 1972-1977*. Wilmington, Del.: Scholarly Resources.

Gans, Herbert J. 1979. *Deciding What's News.* New York: Pantheon.

Germond, Jack W., and Jules Witcover. 1981. *Blue Smoke and Mirrors.* New York: Viking Press.

Gosnell, Harold F. 1937. *Machine Politics Chicago Model.* Chicago: University of Chicago Press.

Greenberg, Bradley S. 1964. "Person-to-person communication in the diffusion of news events." *Journalism Quarterly* 41: 489ff.

Joslyn, Richard, and Janet Johnson. 1982. *Belief and Attitude Change During the 1980 Presidential Campaign.* Washington: American Political Science Association.

Key, V.O. *Public Opinion and American Democracy.* New York: Knopf, 1961.

Kraus, Sidney, ed. 1962. *The Great Debates.* Bloomington: Indiana University Press.

Lazarsfeld, Paul F., and Robert K. Merton. 1971. "Mass communication, popular taste, and organized social action." In *The Process and Effects of Mass Communication,* edited by Wilbur Schramm and Donald F. Roberts. Urbana: University of Illinois Press.

Lippmann, Walter. 1920. *Liberty and the News.* New York: Harcourt, Brace and Howe.

Matthews, Donald R. 1978. "'Winnowing': The news media and the 1976 presidential nominations." In *Race for the Presidency,* edited by James David Barber. Englewood Cliffs: Prentice-Hall.

Nie, Norman H., Sidney Verba, and John R. Petrocik. 1976. *The Changing American Voter.* Cambridge: Harvard University Press.

Park, Robert E. 1929. *The Immigrant Press and Its Control.* New York: Harper and Brothers.

Polsby, Nelson, and Aaron Wildavsky. 1976. *Presidential Elections.* New York: Charles Scribner's Sons.

Robinson, John. 1972. "Perceived media bias and the 1968 vote." *Journalism Quarterly* 49: 239ff.

Robinson, John. 1974. "The press as king maker." *Journalism Quarterly* 51: 587ff.

Robinson, Michael J. 1976. "Public affairs television and the growth of political malaise." *Americao Political Science Review* 69: 409ff.

Robinson, Michael J. 1977. "Television and American politics: 1956-1976." *The Public Interest* 48: 3ff.

Royko, Mike. 1971. *Boss.* New York: Signet.

Schiller, Herbert I. 1973. *The Mind Managers.* Boston: Beacon Press.

Sigal, Leon. 1973. *Reporters and Officials.* Lexington, Mass: D.C. Heath.

Smith, Stephen, and Elizabeth Rudulph. 1980. "A convention hall of mirrors." *Time*, 28 July 1980, p. 54ff.

Taylor, Garth, James Davis, and John Fry. 1976. *User's Instructions for the DTSS Program IMPLIB***:CATFIT*. Hanover: Department of Sociology, Dartmouth College.

Tichenor, P.J., G.A. Donohue, and C.N. Olien. 1970. "Mass media flow and differential growth in knowledge." Public Opinion Quarterly 34: 159ff.

Verba, Sidney, and Norman H. Nie. 1972. *Participation in America*. New York: Harper and Row.

Warwick, Donald P., and Charles A. Lininger. 1975. *The Sample Survey: Theory and Practice*. New York: McGraw Hill.

Weisberg, Herbert F., and Bruce D. Bowen. 1979. *An Introduction to Survey Research and Data Analysis*. San Francisco: W.H. Freeman and Company.

White, Theodore H. 1969. *The Making of the President 1968*. New York: Atheneum.

Witcover, Jules. 1978. *Marathon*. New York: Signet.

Yule, G. Udny, and M.G. Kendall. 1950. *An Introduction to the Theory of Statistics*. London; Charles Griffin.

NOTES